My SMART ROMANCE

A True Story and Poems

by

Terri Lynn Smart Packard

ISBN 979-8-89112-898-9 (Paperback)
ISBN 979-8-89112-899-6 (Digital)

Copyright © 2024 Terri Lynn Smart Packard
All rights reserved
First Edition

All rights reserved. No part of this publication may be reproduced, distributed, or transmitted in any form or by any means, including photocopying, recording, or other electronic or mechanical methods without the prior written permission of the publisher. For permission requests, solicit the publisher via the address below.

Covenant Books
11661 Hwy 707
Murrells Inlet, SC 29576
www.covenantbooks.com

CONTENTS

Chapter 1: Giving Up My Dream 1
    Recipe for Cornflake Chicken 10
Chapter 2: Our Meeting 11
    Recipe for Hawaiian Chicken 21
Chapter 3: First Date 22
    Recipe for Goulash 28
Chapter 4: Will There Be a Second Date? 29
    Recipe for Nut Goodie Bars 38
Chapter 5: Engagement 39
    Recipe for Joan's Salsa 48
Chapter 6: Planning for a Wedding 49
    Recipe for Tuna Salad 55
Chapter 7: Cards and More Cards 56
    Recipe for Strawberry Jell-O Cake 66
Chapter 8: Cooking 67
    Recipe for Pepper Steak and Rice 72
Chapter 9: Spring and Easter 74
    Recipe for Deviled Eggs 80
Chapter 10: Counseling 81
    Recipe for Dump in the Pan Chocolate Cake 86
Chapter 11: Fixing Up Our New Home 87
    Recipe for Beef Stroganoff 94
Chapter 12: Showers and Rehearsal 95
    Recipe for Evelyn's Jell-O 105
Chapter 13: The Wedding 106
    Recipe for Raisin Rocks 113

Chapter 14: The Reception..114
    Recipe for Grandma Smart's Homemade Egg Noodles.........118
Chapter 15: Honeymoon..120
    Recipe for Honeymoon Salad..130

Epilogue...131

CHAPTER 1

Giving Up My Dream

Adorned in a flowing white wedding gown with a lacy veil covering my happy face, I swept down the aisle of the church surrounded by flowers. At the altar, there stood this strikingly handsome prince of a man. Our eyes met, and the lightning of love flashed between us.

That was my dream as a young woman. I went to a Christian college, looking for the hunk who loved Jesus. Turned out, I studied a lot more than I dated. I loved the dorm life, the campus, the classes, but where was that guy? After four years, I graduated with honors, a bachelor of arts degree, and a teaching license in math and science, but no engagement ring.

So I went to graduate school. I was in a new state and a new city—Pittsburgh, Pennsylvania. I started my new life in my first apartment. Maybe here was where my prince was hiding.

Dear Lord,

Create in me a person who can fill the place
in life You have prepared for me.
Amen.

I was a graduate assistant at the University of Pittsburgh. That meant I got my tuition at graduate school and a minuscule stipend to live on. In exchange for this, I was to teach several Chemistry 101 labs to college freshmen who knew next to nothing about chemistry. I set up the laboratory, coached the students through the lab, and graded their lab reports. I also proctored their exams. I had to watch out for those cheaters.

The week classes started at the University of Pittsburgh, booths were set up around campus to get students involved in different groups and activities. One table sold student-priced tickets to the Pittsburgh Symphony and the Pittsburgh Opera. I thought the tickets were a great price at twenty-five dollars each. I also thought I would love to see an opera and hear some good music, so I purchased the season passes. Before each symphony or opera, I was sent a synopsis that explained about the upcoming program. That helped a lot since the operas were not in English. My seats were not the best; they were in the "nosebleed" section. I was able to attend six symphonies and five operas. The symphonies were directed by Andre Previn. I was supposed to see Itzhak Perlman in November, but he had to cancel his appearance. That was a bummer. The operas were *The Bartered Bride, Rigoletto, Faust, Fidelio,* and *Manon LeScaut.* I enjoyed going to these performances, but I was going alone. I wished someone was with me to enjoy the performances, then I could talk to someone about the music.

My graduate classes in chemistry were interesting. I had to study a lot, so I got passing grades. One day, I was feeling lonely and homesick. I was sitting outside, enjoying a bird singing while I ate my lunch, and a group of students came out onto the patio. I thought, *Oh no, I do not want to be around a lot of party people.* Boy, was I wrong. This was a group of Christian graduate students who met once a week for Bible study and prayer. This was the only time all year that they ever met outside. God directed our paths to cross. I would never have known there was such a group in the large science building. I was so glad to find other scientists who knew Jesus as their Savior. I attended every study with them after I found the group.

I joined Dr. Asher's laboratory group. This gave me a small desk in the Chemistry Building on the ninth floor that I could call my own. In Dr. Asher's group, we were studying the chemical bonds in hemoglobin. We used a laser directed at our samples to measure bond

MY SMART ROMANCE

lengths and how they vibrated. Dr. Asher was a short, round man, who always had a pipe in his mouth even though it was seldom lit. His group had one recent PhD recipient and four or five of us, grad students, working toward our doctorates.

The lab group knew I was a Christian, so I was scrutinized. I was questioned about life and my walk with the Lord.

"Why don't you drink?" they asked. I tried to explain that my body was the temple of the Holy Spirit. I was committed to keep my body pure (*no* smoking, *no* drugs, *no* alcohol, *no* sex outside marriage). I didn't even use bad language. They thought I was weird.

I prayed.

Dear Lord,

May I know how to speak in wisdom about Christ. He has done so much for me. I have to share it. Make me a branch that bears fruit and can be profitable to You! Help me to abide in You. I know, Lord, that without You, I can do nothing.

Love,
Terri

Dr. Asher was to speak at a conference at Ohio State University, so he took our whole laboratory group with him. We stayed in the college dorms. The room had only a bunk bed and two desks. I was surprised there were no sheets or blankets on the beds. I did not know I would need bedding.

Our group went out to a fancy restaurant the first night in Columbus. There was octopus on the salad bar, so I tried it for the first time. It was like chewing rubber bands and tasted like rubber bands—definitely not my favorite.

I was interested in seeing Columbus and Ohio State University. My father had attended and graduated from Ohio State University.

I had been born in Columbus, Ohio. On a chilly October morning, Ila Smart was up early. She was getting everything ready

3

for her husband, Ira, to go to work. But Ila stopped the preparations and went to the bedroom. She told Ira, "You don't need to go to work today. Our baby is going to come soon."

Ira Smart jumped out of bed and ran around wildly. He was so excited. He tried to grab the prepared suitcase and rush to the hospital. Ila calmly told him he could get dressed first before they went.

A short time later Ila, Ira, and Bessie, Ira's sister, all got in the car. It was a forty-mile drive to Columbus, where the hospital was located. When they arrived at the hospital, Ila was seen by a doctor. After he examined her, he said, "Go home! You are not going to have this baby today."

Well, Ila knew differently. She did not want to drive forty miles home to have to rush back to Columbus again. She, Ira, and Bessie went downtown Columbus to look in the shops. They stayed in all the big department stores like Lazarus. They believed that if the baby was born in one of the big stores, they would receive a free layette for the baby.

Every five minutes, Ila grabbed a counter as she had a contraction pain. Ira and Bessie just walked on down the aisle and pretended not to know her. Finally, the contractions were strong enough and close enough together for Ila to go back to the hospital.

They all got back in their car to return to Doctors Hospital. Ila lay on the front seat, tired out from all the walking. At an intersection, a potato chip delivery truck ran into their car. They could not continue to the hospital. When the police arrived at the scene, Ira frantically told them his wife was about to have a baby in the car.

So the police sounded their sirens and flashed their lights as Ira followed through the city traffic to the hospital. When they arrived at the hospital, all Ila wanted to do was go to sleep on the seat of the car. She kept saying, "Just let me rest." But Bessie and Ira hurried her into the hospital.

Ila was taken to a delivery room. Ira and Bessie were shown to a waiting room. The pair anxiously waited for news of the impending arrival. Finally, a nurse carried a little girl straight from the delivery room to her father. Ira was shocked and thought something was terribly wrong. The baby, me, had not been cleaned up after delivery. I

MY SMART ROMANCE

was shown to my father all bloody and messy. The nurse assured Ira that everything was just fine. So on October 23, 1959, Terri Lynn Smart arrived in this world. Here I am.

After the science symposiums that Professor Asher spoke at, he said we were all going to a social function with a keg. I told him I would not be attending. Dr. Asher said it was how I would meet other scientists and make connections. I explained that I thought the emphasis on alcohol was not needed to meet people and make good connections for my studies and experiments. He allowed me to skip the function.

I was not the only female in this lab family. There were two other women. A third-year graduate student was a lovely young lady, who invited me to her home. She still lived with her parents in Pittsburgh. She was a very slender person, with health and stomach issues. She followed a very limited diet so she would not be ill. At her home, I saw loads of trophies. There were beautiful pictures of her wearing dazzling costumes on the ice alone and in pair's competition. She had skated all her life. I wondered why she was studying chemistry. Later she quit the study of science, joined the *Disney on Ice* show, and skated out of my life.

The third female in our group was also a first-year grad student like me. She wore bib overalls and had a huge German Shepherd dog. The dog was for protection because she was living alone in a not-so-nice part of the city. She was very down-to-earth and friendly. She taught me to make oven-fried chicken with a cornflake coating. After I left Pittsburgh, she sent me a photo of her wedding. It was a large Polish Catholic wedding. The bride's maids wore national Polish dresses with white aprons and wreaths in their hair with red ribbons floating down their backs.

My apartment was in a suburb of Pittsburgh. It was a one-bedroom with one bath in the basement of a small three-story apartment building. I had a woodstove in the living room. There were shelves covering one whole wall of the bedroom. I had the luxury of a huge walk-in closet for my clothes. I also had a place to park my car behind the apartment. I could enter my apartment through the back door. I did not have to park on the street or go in and out the front with the other tenants.

The apartment was heated by electric baseboard heaters. I could not afford to pay the high electric bills in the winter, so I tried to not turn on the heaters. I tried to heat my rooms with the woodstove, but it smoked and would not stay lit. So I slept with a lot of blankets on my single bed. I would jump out of bed in the morning and race into the hot shower. The hot water would steam up the bathroom. After the shower, I would throw on my clothes quickly before I got chilled. Next, I would have breakfast of cereal and milk.

I drove to the university campus each day. It was about five miles from my apartment. I would try and find parking on the streets near the chemistry building. Parking was at a premium. One day, street cleaning day, I found a choice spot on a street that had already been cleaned. When I returned to my car, I had a ticket under my windshield wiper. I had parked in that spot thirty minutes before the allowed time. I started looking for parking above the science building. The building had a tall cliff behind it. There were houses on the streets above. Most days I found a spot up there and had to walk down a long staircase to the back of my building. Walking down the steep stairs was a little scary, but walking up after a day of work and study was a real chore.

Another day, heading from my car toward the stairs, there was a colored man walking toward me. He was dressed in a trench coat and carrying a paper lunch bag in both hands in front of him. As I drew near on the sidewalk, he moved the paper bag to reveal his unclothed "package." I quickly got away and down the stairs. When I got to my lab, I was laughing about being flashed. Dr. Asher did not think it was funny. He made special arrangements and paid for me to have a parking pass in the university parking lot of our building.

I have always loved going to church. I love the music, the sermons, the Bible study, and the fellowship. I started looking for a church to attend right after I moved to Pittsburgh. I took out the phone book and started looking for Baptist churches. The first one I visited left a big impression on me. I parked my car and walked across the street to be greeted by two beautiful Black women, dressed

MY SMART ROMANCE

in white dresses and white gloves. They helped me find a seat in the filling up sanctuary. When I looked around at the congregation, I noticed I was the only White person in the crowd. I had a nice time that Sunday, but I felt out of place. I did not think this was the church for me.

The next Sunday, I tried the next church in the phone book. I found a small church, like my home church in Virginia. I attended Swissvale Baptist Church all the time I lived in Pittsburgh. A young man from my hometown started to attend Carnegie Mellon University in Pittsburgh that fall. I volunteered to pick him up on Sundays for church. Attending the church service caused him to miss his lunch at his college. I volunteered to feed him lunch after church then take him back to his campus. He invited a roommate to join us, and then another college student joined us. Usually, there were four of us for lunch at my little apartment after the Sunday morning service. One Sunday, the church had a special visiting preacher, Jack Keep. I volunteered to feed him lunch with my other boys. Later, Pastor Keep became the pastor of my home church in Virginia.

> Close to thee,
> Oh, my Savior,
> I long to be.
> But I soon fall,
> And slip away
> In no time at all.
> How can I stay close
> To You, Lord,
> Now and always?

As a preteen and teen, I had always been on a Bible quiz team. I had even won a leather-bound Scofield Bible for being the top "Quiz-er." I volunteered to coach the Bible quiz team for the Swissvale Baptist Church. The teenagers on the team and I met on Wednesday nights while the adults had a prayer meeting. I wrote out questions about the Bible passage to be covered by the competition, and the contestants practiced answering quickly. Once a month, we had a youth rally. We met at different churches around the Pittsburgh area. We had the quiz first then a message and finished the rally with refreshments. I do not remember our team winning, but we did have a good time.

I love to sing praises to God, so I joined the church choir. We practiced right before the Sunday evening preaching service. Every Sunday, the choir sang for the congregation during the morning worship service. One Sunday, I and another female choir member sang "I Come to the Garden Alone" as a special number.

Most Sundays, after the evening church service, the Hill family invited me to their home for a time of fellowship. Three generations lived in their four-story home. We had fun and would watch TV together. I did not have a TV in my apartment, so it was a nice diversion. They always fed me a light supper. The Hill family became like my adopted family.

The father, Tom Hill, had only one leg. Years before, he had stopped on the highway to help a motorist with a flat tire, and a passing truck hit him. The accident caused him to lose the leg below the knee. He wore a wooden leg when he was at church. But as soon as he was home, off came the wooden leg, and he used crutches to get around. You could see the leg standing alone in the corner.

I thought I would be living in Pittsburgh for at least four years while I attended graduate school.

So when my driver's license needed renewal, I got a Pennsylvania one. Then I took my car to the Pennsylvania inspection station so I could get Pennsylvania tags. But the car brakes failed to pass the test. What could I do? Well, the men at my church told me it was an easy fix. They said I could fix the brakes myself. So I borrowed a garage from a church member, and I replaced my front brakes all by myself. I was told, to fix the rear brakes, all you had to do was drive backward and slam on the brakes. So I went to an empty bank parking lot and put my car in reverse and then quickly put on the brakes a couple of times. I took the car back to the inspection station, and it passed. I got my Pennsylvania car tags.

At the University of Pittsburgh, I experimented in a darkened laboratory. I was shooting my colorful laser beams across a prepared sample of hemoglobin. I hoped to examine the rotation of the bonds in the sample. I spent many hours trying to get some results. Sitting in the dark, I thought, *Do I really want this life? I feel confined and imprisoned in this dark room.*

None of my experiments gave me any usable data. Nothing I did worked. Dr. Asher told me to go ahead and write up the experiment, as if it had worked. He said he was sure the results would turn out the way he expected. So he said I should write an article for a scientific journal. He believed it would be good because we needed women in science to publish. His group could get more grant money if we published. I refused to write and publish something that was not true. The experiments did not prove what he wanted me to write. I felt betrayed by the scientific community. Scientists could publish articles that were so colored by their own beliefs but were not supported by their experiments did not seem right. They could make their data prove any point they wanted. I still have skepticism about what the experts say science proves.

That was when I started to think that pure experimental science and the pursuit of a PhD was not for me. I had a full life in Pittsburgh, but where did God want me? Near the end of that first year, I was praying for God's leading. I felt I should be using my teaching license. I called my home church, Evangel Baptist Church, which had a Christian school. I talked to the principal, and they needed a high school teacher for science and math. After I interviewed with them, I was hired. I was on my way back home to Virginia. I was twenty-three years old and was starting a new career.

I told God I would be an "Old Maid" schoolteacher for Him.

Recipe for Cornflake Chicken

Ingredients:

- 3/4 cup cornflake crumbs
- 1 egg
- 1 cup milk
- 1 cup all-purpose flour
- 1/2 teaspoon salt
- 1/4 teaspoon pepper
- about a 3-pound chicken, cut in pieces, rinsed, and dried
- 3 tablespoons melted butter

Directions:

1. Preheat oven to 350 degrees Fahrenheit.
2. Place cornflake crumbs in shallow dish. Set aside.
3. In small mixing bowl, beat egg and milk slightly. Add flour, salt, and pepper. Mix till smooth.
4. Dip chicken in batter.
5. Coat with cereal.
6. Place in single layer, skin side up in foil-lined shallow baking pan.
7. Drizzle with butter.
8. Bake one hour or until chicken is tender, no longer pink, and juices run clear. Do not cover pan or turn chicken while baking.

While living in Pittsburgh, I learned how to cut a whole chicken up into pieces. I felt so accomplished.

CHAPTER 2

Our Meeting

I loved moving back home. I had a large bedroom in the basement of my parents' home. I had a bathroom all to myself. My mom cooked dinner for Dad and me every night. I always got along well with my parents so, it was great to be home. I only paid my parents a hundred dollars a month for rent. I had it made.

Dear Lord,

    Thank You for my parents. Their love for me is so great. I need their love. They have taught me Your Word. They have been an example to me. They care about things in my life. I love them very much. Watch over them this day, and help them to grow closer to You.
    In Jesus's name,
    Amen.

Home is a happy place to live.
Haunted with friendly ghost of memory.
Filled with love and harmony
Expectant with hopes and promises.

I was excited about the beginning of the school year. Evangel Baptist Church had kindergarten to twelfth grade in their Christian school. My high school best friend, Shawne, was also going to teach at the school. She was a first-grade teacher, and I was going to teach high school classes.

Lord,

Help my teaching to never become just a job. Help me to use it as a ministry and opportunity to build into young lives. Help me to direct their feet in the paths of righteousness.
Amen.

That summer, before school started, Shawne and I planned a progressive dinner for our college- and career-age Sunday school class. For a progressive dinner, you have each course of the meal at a different home. Someone made soup at the first house. Then we went to another house for salad. The next course of vegetables was served at another house. The main dish was eaten somewhere else. Finally, dessert was served at the last home.

Shawne and I were going to cook the main dish, Hawaiian Chicken. She had found the recipe in a magazine. Shawne came to my house because my mother had two ovens in her kitchen. We started cooking. Well, this was summer in Northern Virginia, and it was hot and humid. As we used the two ovens, the house got hotter and hotter. The air conditioner was not keeping up with the heat. When we were finished cooking the Hawaiian Chicken, Shawne and I left and took the chicken to the house where the main course was to be served. My parents came home, and the house was so hot; they could not stay there. They had to go out to dinner and stay out of the house till after dark, when the house finally cooled down some.

I was setting up my classroom at the school. It was a new room in a brand-new multipurpose gym attached to the church. The science room had two raised benches for doing experiments with a sink on the end of each bench. Bunsen burner gas connectors and electric

MY SMART ROMANCE

plugs were located in the center of the countertops. This room was so much better than the science classrooms I had when I went to Engleside Christian High School in Alexandria, Virginia. I remember doing physics experiments in a little closet in the basement of Engleside Baptist Church. We would time how long it took for a little car on wheels to race down a track we had made and figure out the velocity. Mr. Rich was my high school physics teacher. He modeled for me how to be a good science teacher.

My parents came to the school and laid down the tile on the cement floor of the new science classroom. That was a big help to the school and me. The room would be ready to use on the very first day of school. What a blessing to have a new room in a new school for this new teacher.

I was to teach earth science to eighth graders, physical science to ninth graders, biology to tenth graders, and chemistry to eleventh and twelfth graders. I also had a pre-algebra class and study hall for the eighth graders. I had a full teaching day. I had a lot of planning and preparation for each class. We did not have computers or word processors or even a copy machine at the school. I did have a top-of-the-line calculator that cost me a small fortune. Now everyone can get that same calculator for about twenty dollars.

I had to use a typewriter to type my notes and test for each class on mimeograph paper. If I made a typo on the paper, I had to use a knife and scrap off the mistake. What a pain! After the paper was typed, I hooked it into a mimeograph machine. Then I had to turn a crank to copy each page separately. This was a very time-consuming enterprise.

I used an overhead projector in my classroom. I was very modern. No chalkboard writing for me. I projected the notes on the front screen as I wrote them on a plastic sheet. My students copied the notes and kept them in a science notebook. I could face the class as I wrote, which kept their misdeeds to a minimum. There still could be notes passed and spitballs thrown. Students in a Christian school do not all act like saints.

Each teacher at the school was in charge of a homeroom. Homeroom was where the middle school and high school students started their day. I was assigned the eighth-grade homeroom with eighteen students. We had a small room with three rows of desks. There was hardly any room to walk between the desks. The desks were the kind with a chair having storage under it and hooked to a writing surface. In the morning, I took attendance and lunch orders. We said the Pledge of Allegiance to the American flag. Each day, I prayed for a blessed day and any request the students would share. Then a bell would ring, and the students would scatter their various ways to class. I had to hurry to another building to get to my science laboratory. Then at lunchtime, the eighth graders and I would return to the tiny homeroom for our lunch. The teachers ate lunch with their class. This allowed teachers to listen to and mentor their students.

One Monday, a young girl in my homeroom came in, spouting out how she hated going to church. She hated Sunday school. I asked if she had been saved. She said, "Sure." I asked her if she hated the Bible, God's Word? Did she hate worshipping God? If she hated all those things, maybe she needed to check whether she actually had asked Jesus to be her Savior. Jesus Christ wants us to love Him, love His Word, and love our Christian brothers and sisters. Years later, this girl grew up to be a wonderful wife and mother. She and I are friends on Facebook. She is constantly sharing Bible verses on Facebook. She loves Jesus and her church now.

Things were going great at school. I enjoyed teaching. I felt I was using my God-given talents. The students were held to a high academic standard in my classes. I gave out notes each day. Preparing for a chapter test, I would spend a whole day in class reviewing the material to be covered on the test.

After a test, I would go over the answers to the test so students who missed something could write in the correct answer. When an exam was scheduled, I explained that all the questions would come directly from their chapter test. I required the students to keep a notebook with a section for notes, homework, quizzes, and tests. At each exam time, I collected the notebooks and gave an extra test grade for how well they kept their notebooks.

MY SMART ROMANCE

My life was enriched by coaching. I was the girls' volleyball coach in the fall and the softball coach in the spring. We had to travel quite a distance to get to play other Christian schools in our league. It was fun to be active. I liked helping the girls learn to play better and learn to be good sports.

My grandmother, Cassie Johnston, was visiting us in Virginia from her home in Minnesota. When I was young, my favorite place was Grandma Cassie's house. My grandma was such a special lady. She would make you feel loved and secure. Her house was always warm and welcoming. My grandma lived in a place called Boy River, Minnesota. It was two hundred miles north of the Twin Cities. There were lots of trees and lakes around Grandma's place. It could be a very cold place in the winter.

One Christmas, before I started school, we made the long, long trip from our home in New Jersey to Grandma's house in Northern Minnesota. We had a wonderful time at Grandma's house. My sister and I played in the snow. We went sliding, made snow angels and snowmen. When we would come in to Grandma's after playing, we had wonderful things to eat. Grandma would let us go to the basement and look at the shelves full of home canned goods. We were allowed to pick out any canned goods we wanted to eat. I had two absolute favorites: first, Grandma's homemade dill pickles. I could eat a whole jar of them all by myself. My other favorite was Grandma's raspberry sauce. She grew her own raspberries and made the best sauce.

The day after New Year's Day, we were to leave Grandma's. We had to pack up the car and start for home early in the morning. I could not bear to leave. I did not want to leave Grandma's house and my grandma.

When I got in the car, I started praying silently.

Dear Lord,

Please don't let us go home. Let us go back to Grandma's house.

As I sat in the back seat a weeping bundle, my father was struggling to drive in a blizzard. The snowdrifts were getting deeper and deeper. The car engine struggled to work against the snow. Only two miles from Grandma's house, Daddy had to stop the car. He got out in the blowing snow and opened the car hood. He looked under the hood. Snow was packed inside all around the engine. When he got back into the car, he said, "We will have to turn around. We can't make it in this weather."

I perked right up. My tears were gone. I started to sing praises to God. Jesus had answered my prayer. Oh, I was so happy.

"Jesus loves me this I know!" I sang.

My mother looked back at me and asked, "Why are you so happy?"

I answered, "God answered my prayer!"

She then asked me, "What was your prayer?"

I said, "That I would not have to leave Grandma."

My mother then explained to me that we had to get home because Daddy had to go to work. We were a family and should pray together, *not* against each other. The things we pray for should not be selfish things.

When we arrived at Grandma's house, I ran into her soft wrinkled arms and hugged her. I kissed her soft wrinkled neck and face. I was so glad to be back with her.

In a few hours, the snowplow drove by the house. The plow cleared all the deep snow off the road. Then my family had to get back in the car. We started the trip home to New Jersey all over again.

I was a little sad, but I felt better about leaving. I prayed with my family that we would have a safe trip home.

God hears our every prayer. He answers them all. But they are answered in different ways.

Sometimes God gives us what we ask for. When we had to go back to Grandma's, He gave me what I asked. Sometimes God says, "No" because something is not good for us. Then sometimes God says, "Wait. I have a better plan." God knows what is best for each of us. We must have faith in His goodness and always pray without ceasing.

MY SMART ROMANCE

One morning, in November of 1983, while visiting my family in Virginia, Grandma Cassie fell unconscious in our bathroom. Her body was wedged between the tub and the toilet. We had to call 911 for an ambulance. They rushed my grandmother to the closest hospital. A bleed in her brain had caused her to have a stroke. Slowly, her brain shut down. They transferred her to another hospital better equipped to deal with strokes and brain injuries. I sat with her in that hospital's intensive care unit. I did not know if she heard me, but I sang hymns and read the twenty-third Psalm to her. She died in the Alexandria Hospital on November 13, 1983. Her body was flown to Minnesota.

> But He knoweth the way that I take: When He hath tried me, I shall come forth as gold. (Job 23:10)

> Pure and bright
> Is the gold after the fire.
> The time and heat
> Increase its value.
> So a Christian is improved
> By testings and trials.

My family drove to Minnesota for her funeral. My parents were staying up there to take care of Grandma Cassie's estate, but I had to return to my teaching job. So I had to fly back to Northern Virginia alone.

As my flight was descending, approaching the Washington National Airport, the airplane suddenly shot back up in the air. My stomach felt like it was in my mouth. I was so scared. On my mind was the recent TV news story that showed the Air Florida Flight 90 airplane crashing into the Fourteenth Street Bridge over the Potomac River while taking off from Washington National Airport. The older man sitting next to me could see my terror. He asked, "Would it help if I held your hand?"

I nodded my head in agreement and, with a quavering voice, said, "Yes."

So all during the landing, I was holding this stranger's hand. It really was a comfort. When we landed, I thanked him for his kindness. My parents returned to Virginia at the beginning of December.

I had attended Evangel Baptist Church since I was young, and I was very familiar with the building. The main entrance had huge colonial looking columns holding up the portico. When entering the doors, you would arrive in the foyer. Ahead on both the right and left side were double doors into the sanctuary. The church did not have a central aisle; there were two aisles one on each side, dividing the pews into three sections: middle, left, and right. The pulpit was in the center on a raised platform. Behind the pulpit were two rows of chairs for the choir. Above the heads of the choir members was the baptismal area. The back of the baptismal pool was painted with a lovely pastoral scene. There was an organ to the right of the platform and a piano on the left side. Everything was painted white with gold trim: the walls, the pews, the pulpit, and the privacy fence in front of the choir loft. It looked majestic. The side walls had huge two-story-tall windows in a purple tinted glass that glowed when the sun shone through. I loved my church in Dale City, Virginia.

Attending church was the center of my family's life. Before I started school, my family moved to New Jersey from Minnesota. We lived in a place called Dover. We attended the First Baptist Church of Dover. Every Sunday, you could find the Smart family sitting three pews from the front on the left-hand side of the church. One Sunday, my mother was intently listening to the preacher as he delivered his sermon. Well, I was very bored! So I slipped off the pew onto the floor. My mother did not get upset with me or say anything. (She probably did not notice.) So I stayed down there on the floor.

Well, I was still bored, so I started crawling under the seats from one row to the next. As a little girl, this was extremely easy to do. Everything looked different from the floor. Under the pews was not boring!

When I was very little, I really liked purses. I would carry one around the house all the time. I could pack them full of interesting things. Well, on the floor of that church were all kinds of purses. I started collecting the purses off the floor. I would crawl back to

MY SMART ROMANCE

mother's row and leave the purses, then I would crawl away and pick up a few more purses. I would put them all at my mother's feet.

When my mother finally looked down, I had quite a nice group of purses at her feet. How embarrassed my mother was. She had to return all those purses to the right ladies after the final prayer at church.

On the trip home from church, I was lectured on how to behave in the Lord's house. I was informed that stealing was a sin. Taking other people's purses was stealing. I was also told I had to sit on the pew during the whole service. I was to sit right between my mother and father each Sunday in church and stay there.

My family went every time the church doors were open. We went Sundays to Sunday school, worship service, choir practice, and evening worship service. On Wednesday nights, we attended prayer meetings. We only missed church if we were very sick. When our family traveled, we always looked for a church to attend on Sundays. We believed the Bible's injunction in Hebrews, "Not to forsake the assembling together." My father was a deacon at the church. We always sat in the center section of pews on the third row all my life. It was as if our family name was written on that pew. One time we even walked as a family to church in the snow because the roads were not passable for our car.

After Christmas break, my first year teaching at Evangel Christian School, we were halfway through the school year. All the teachers and students were charged up to get back to work. The first Wednesday night in January 1984, my parents and I were running late for prayer meeting, so instead of walking up front to our pew during the beginning of the service, we sat near the back on the right side. It felt a little strange because we were not in our normal place. Things looked different from this side of the church and not from the middle. You could see the back of many people's heads.

At the end of the service, Pastor Gelina called on a young man to close in prayer. The young man was not someone from our church. The young man was visiting our church with his friend and mentor, a retired pastor named Bill McLean. I could see the back of his head as he sat in the middle section in front of where I was sitting. He was well-dressed in a suit and tie. He did not mind closing the service in prayer.

As people were leaving the sanctuary, I approached the visiting young man. I wanted to invite him to our College and Career Sunday school class. I introduced myself. "Hi, I'm Terri Smart."

He introduced himself as Larry Packard. He was a very handsome fellow, with dark brown hair, blue eyes, and a fine mustache. We talked for about five minutes. Then Larry asked, "Are you married?"

I was a little taken aback by that question. But I answered, "No."

We talked for a few minutes more, and Larry asked me, "Can I have your phone number?" Wow, no guy had ever asked me for my phone number before. I felt honored and excited. I gave Larry my number. This was before cell phones. So the number was my parents' home phone number.

We walked out of the sanctuary into the foyer of the church. My parents were waiting for me out there and talking to other church members. I introduced Larry Packard to my parents. He shook their hands, and we all walked out of the church to our cars.

I rode home with my parents. From the back seat of their car, I told my parents about Larry asking if I was married and then asking for my phone number.

Much later, Larry explained to me that he had set a rule for himself not to talk very long with married ladies. He did not want to be inappropriate. He wanted to protect himself and his reputation. He wanted to be pure before the Lord.

Larry was riding with his friends, the McLeans, after that Wednesday night prayer meeting.

When Larry got in that car with Pastor and Mrs. McLean the night we met, he said, "Maybe I made a mistake. I asked a woman for her phone number."

The McLeans asked who he had talked to. When he told them who he had talked to, they shared about my family and assured Larry it was an appropriate thing to do.

So my advice for meeting single handsome men who love the Lord, go to prayer meetings.

20

Recipe for Hawaiian Chicken

Ingredients:

- 12 chicken pieces
- 1 bottle Catalina dressing
- 1 envelope onion soup mix
- 1 can pineapple chunks, drained

Directions:

1. Stir dressing and onion soup together.
2. Place chicken pieces in a 9×13-inch pan.
3. Pour dressing over, and toss in pineapple.
4. Bake covered for 45 minutes at 350 degrees.
5. Uncover and bake an additional 30 minutes, basting 2 times.
6. Serve with rice.

CHAPTER 3

First Date

Well, Larry kept me waiting for his call. After three days, I was certain he would never call.

Why would he ask for my number and not call? I gave it up to the Lord. His will was what I wanted in my life.

When Larry finally called, I had to talk to him on the wall phone in my parents' kitchen. Mom was there, cooking goulash for dinner. She answered the phone, and Larry asked to speak to me. Mom called me up from my room on the lower floor of our split-level home.

Larry asked, "Would you go out to dinner with me on Friday night?"

I accepted his invitation.

Then he said, "I will pick you up at seven on Friday. I have a yellow Z28 Camaro."

After I hung up, I told my mother about the upcoming date. I whined, "And he has a yellow Camaro." I was not impressed by fancy cars. My younger sister had a Camaro and was into fancy fast cars, but not me. I like practical cars. My small blue car had a nice economical four-cylinder engine. I thought maybe this guy and I would not get along.

After teaching school on Friday, I prepared for my first date with Larry. I had a bath and fixed my brown, curly hair. I chose a cute dress, pantyhose, and pair of cute high-heeled shoes. A splash of perfume made me feel fancy. I always wore only a little makeup.

MY SMART ROMANCE

Maybe, for my date, I would put on a little eye shadow and lip gloss. I looked into the mirror at myself. My brown eyes stared back at me. My curly, brown hair was at least not sticking out every which way. I thought I looked all right for a first date.

Larry arrived right on time. He was militarily punctual. He rang the doorbell. My father answered the door and invited Larry up to the living room. They sat on the couch and talked for a short time. I soon arrived in the living room, all ready to go out. Larry helped me on with my winter coat.

Then we said good night to my parents.

We started for a nice restaurant called Steak and Ale in Alexandria, Virginia. It was snowing lightly as we left my home in Dale City, Virginia. The drive was about thirty-five minutes down the superhighway I-95 outside Washington, DC.

When we arrived at the restaurant, Larry came around and opened the car door for me. His yellow Z28 Camaro was quite an eye-catcher, but the bucket seats were low. My legs were straight out in front of me. I was not really comfortable riding in his car, and to get out with a dress and high heel on was quite a feat. I tried to be modest as I maneuvered out of his low car.

The interior of the restaurant was dark with stained-glass windows. Each table has a little red candleholder with a flickering candle on the white tablecloth. The furnishings of the restaurant were made of heavy wood. There were dark beams running across the ceilings of each room. A fire blazed in a fireplace, giving a welcoming warm feeling to the place. Pleasant music was quietly playing over the hidden restaurant's speakers. The feel of the whole restaurant was as if I had stepped back in time to an old English tavern.

We had to wait a while for an open table. During the wait, Larry commented on the ring I was wearing. I told Larry about the gold-stone ring I had on. I explained that my parents had given me the ring on my golden birthday. Larry wanted to know what a golden birthday was. I told him it was the one when you were the same age as the number of the day you were born. I was born October 23, and I just had my twenty-third birthday. My sister was born October 21 and had just turned 21. So my parents took the gold-stone earrings of my grandmother Cassie and had them made into rings for each of their daughters. Now my sister and I had matching rings. The rings reminded us of our grandmother Cassie, who had recently gone to heaven.

When we were finally seated, Larry pulled out my chair for me. After consulting the menu, we ordered. Then the two of us got up to go to the salad bar in the next room. The salad plates were in a cooler at the end of the salad bar. They looked like old pewter ware in keeping with the historic theme of the restaurant. There was a wonderful assortment on the salad bar, and we filled our plates.

We returned to our table with our salads. When we were seated, Larry reached over and gently grabbed my hand. I was a little startled. Larry said, "In my family, we always hold hands when we pray before meals." That made me feel a little better about his quick move. Then we bowed our heads, and Larry prayed for our dinner.

We were on our best behavior on this first date. Larry had excellent table manners. Later I learned that I had an earlier girlfriend of his to thank for that. She had instructed Larry on how to hold his utensils correctly. She taught him not to hold his fork or spoon in his fist and not to use them as shovels.

Larry told me he was a heavy mobile mechanic. He worked at Fort Belvoir, Virginia, on the army base. Larry learned to fix tanks when he was in the U. S. Army. He was now a civilian contractor for the army. Well, when I was in college, my father had given me this advice: "Marry a mechanic so he can take care of your car." So being a mechanic was something in his favor.

While we were enjoying our meal and talking in the restaurant, the snow continued to fall. When we walked out to the car in the parking lot, the world was a white wonderland. The light from streetlamps sparkled like diamonds on the fresh snow. Larry helped me carefully back into his car. When he got into the Camaro, he cranked up the heater. It was bitterly cold out. I was glad I was wearing my winter coat.

Larry drove carefully down I-95 south. Camaros do not handle very well on snow or ice. Larry kept the speed way down on the highway. The rode conditions had really deteriorated while we were having dinner. I could see Larry's white knuckles as he hung on to the steering wheel. He had his eyes glued to the road. We did little talking on the ride home.

Finally, Larry turned to the right onto my street, Delmar Drive. Slowly, he drove to the top of the hill. Right at the top of that hill was a sign that said, "End of State Maintenance," and it was true. To that point, the street had been treated for ice but not any further. We started rolling slowly down the hill in my suburban neighborhood. The road was sheer ice. We slid sideways and sideswiped a car parked on the side of the road. There was no stopping. We continued the downward slide and hit a second car. Finally, Larry's yellow Camaro came to rest beside the curb. We were about six houses up the street from my home when we stopped.

Larry asked with a concerned voice, "Are you all right?"

I answered, "I am fine."

I got out of the car and told Larry I would walk home from where we were parked. Larry went door-to-door, trying to find the owners of the cars he had hit. He found the two owners and notified them of the accident. He gave them each his insurance information. I walked carefully down the hill in my high heels. I did not walk on the icy sidewalk. I stayed on the grass, where I had some traction in the snow and ice.

When I got home at about ten thirty, my parents were sitting in the living room, reading. They had been watching for us to come home. They had even gone out in front of our house and put ashes from the fireplace on the street. They thought that would help give traction on the ice. They knew the streets were getting bad.

I told them, "We had an accident." In truth, we had experienced two slow-motion crashes. We had creased the driver's side of each of the cars till we came to a rest near the curb. The passenger door of Larry's car had the yellow paint all scrapped up.

Dear Lord,

Thank You for keeping us safe during these accidents.
Amen.

Holy Righteous God who cares,
Enough to hear my prayers.
He sent His Only Son,
The sinless and righteous One,
To die on a Roman Tree,
For wicked sinners, like me.

I hung up my coat in the closet. I hurried to use the bathroom. I had not used the facilities at the restaurant, and I really had to go. Then I sat with my parents and waited for my date to come back to my house. About forty minutes later, our doorbell rang. There was Larry. He came up to the living room. My dad took his coat. Larry sat on the very edge of the easy chair. He looked like he was ready to fly out of there. He felt so sorry and upset at how our first date ended.

My parents, Larry, and I chatted to pass the time. Larry said he would leave whenever a snowplow came down the street. But no snowplow came! At two in the morning, I said good night to my parents and to Larry. I just left Larry with my parents. I went downstairs to my bedroom. I got ready for bed and went to sleep. It was really late for me. I usually went to bed at nine o'clock in the evening.

Larry and my parents continued to sit upstairs in the living room. Finally, my parents told Larry he could sleep in my sister's empty bedroom upstairs across the hall from their master bedroom.

Reluctantly, Larry accepted. All night, Larry lay on top of the bed fully dressed. He even had his shoes still on. He kept listening for the snowplow to come. What an awkward situation he was in.

On Saturday morning, I awoke and got dressed. All I could think about was that my date was still here. He never left. I never got to debrief my first date with my parents. What did my parents think? It all seemed so strange. It sure was not like any date I had been on before.

As I was making my bed, I looked out my window. There was a policeman next to my car.

What was going on? I quickly went out to speak to the policeman. He told me that during the night a car had hit my car. The strange thing was the person who hit my car had run up onto the sidewalk and sideswiped the passenger side of my car. Larry and I had matching cars. His snazzy yellow Camaro Z28 and my little blue Datsun 210 both had the passenger doors messed up.

Finally, after breakfast, Larry was able to get his car up the hill and go home. So our first date came to an end. It was a date not to be forgotten.

I had heard there was something about Friday the thirteenth being bad luck. Maybe there was some truth in it? Was it bad luck or good luck? I believe it God's providence. God was watching out for us. Our first date was *Friday the thirteenth* of January 1984.

On our first date, Larry spent the night, but I never even got a good night kiss.

Recipe for Goulash

Ingredients:

- 1 pound hamburger
- 1/2 cup chopped onion
- 1/2 cup chopped celery
- 1/2 cup chopped green pepper
- 1 teaspoon season salt
- 1/2 teaspoon Italian seasoning
- 1/2 teaspoon black pepper
- 1 can of tomatoes (whole or chopped)
- 2/3 box elbow macaroni

Directions:

1. Cook macaroni according to package directions. Drain.
2. Brown hamburger with the onion, celery, and green pepper.
3. Add spices and tomatoes to hamburger mixture. Simmer for 20 minutes.
4. Mix cooked macaroni into the meat mixture. Heat thoroughly.

CHAPTER 4

Will There Be a Second Date?

After the tragic end to our first date, I never expected to hear from Larry again. Well, Larry must have been a brave man because he did call me the next Wednesday. He asked how I was and then asked me out again. I accepted, and we set up a time, Friday the twentieth of January, for our second date, only a week after our accident.

When we got in his car, Larry gave me a cute stuffed bear, a gift for me on our second date, wow! We went out for pizza. I love the hand-tossed crust at the local pizza place. The pie was loaded with cheese, pepperoni, and sausage. Larry always orders a Pepsi as it is his favorite drink. I just have water. Water may be my favorite drink. We held hands as we prayed before our meal. We bit into the delicious triangles of cheesy goodness. I had to use a lot of napkins.

After we ate, we went back to my house. In the family room, in the basement, my parents had a ping-pong table. We played a rousing game of doubles ping-pong with my parents. Mom and Dad were one team, and Larry and I were the other. I used to play ping-pong against my sister when we were teens. The loser had to do the dinner dishes. So I got pretty good with a ping-pong paddle. I did not want to wash the dishes. Larry had learned to play ping-pong when he was a boy. He attended the Washington, DC, Police Boys' Camp in the summers. Larry became a ping-pong champ there. Boy, he had a great serve, and he could return the ball with a slam. We beat my parents in two out of the three games we played.

29

When it was time for Larry to leave, I walked him to the door. My parents were in another part of the house. Finally, we were alone. As we said good night, Larry gave me my first kiss. He wrapped his arms around me, and our lips met. It was sweet and gentle. His mustache tickled me a little. Then Larry went home, leaving me to cherish that first kiss.

Larry started calling me on the phone every Saturday and Wednesday. He was attending Washington Bible College on Tuesday and Thursday evenings. He wanted to get his Bible degree. He worked all day at Fort Belvoir, fixing trucks. Then he would drive around Washington, DC, to Landover, Maryland, to take his Bible courses in the evening. His favorite professor was Dr. Sam Fowler. He always quotes Dr. Fowler. "Get yourself a pack of 3×5 cards, and write the verses you want to memorize on them. When you have to wait in a line, pull out the cards and review the verses." Another quote from Dr. Fowler: "You think through ink." So Larry always writes down things he wants to remember.

Well, I thought about Larry a lot after that second date. He was five feet, ten inches tall, just about three inches taller than me. I could look up at him. He had a head full of shiny dark hair he wore parted on the right side. His hair waved over his high forehead and down to his collar. His ears just peaked out of the side of his head. His eyes were a beautiful blue that sparkled when he laughed. I enjoyed gazing into them. He had a straight nose and sweet cheeks that dimpled when he smiled. He had a luxurious brown mustache and straight white teeth. I loved to see him smile. His chin was firm with a divot in the middle, like Kirk Douglas's chin. He had nice firm biceps that I thought were exciting. His hands were well manicured, even though he worked as a mechanic in grease and dirt. Other mechanic's hands may have oil embedded in their skin but not Larry's. The mechanics at his shop even asked him how he kept his hands so nice. He worked hard with a nailbrush to care for his hands and nails.

Working on the heavy equipment, Larry had to wear blue work pants and blue shirt. He had heavy steel-toe boots to protect his feet. So when he was not at work, Larry always dressed impeccably. He had all his dress shirts professionally pressed and starched. He had very handsome outfits. His dress shoes were always spit shinned in a military manner. I thought he was handsome from head to toe.

The next Sunday, it snowed. So after morning church, all the single female teachers from the school decided to go sliding. We all bundled up in layers of our warmest clothes. The hill at the local middle school, which I had attended as a young girl, was perfect for sliding. What fun to go swishing down the hill! Our faces turned rosy from the cold and exercise. It was great to have such good Christian friends.

> Friends are the people Who…
> Sing with you when you are happy.
> Cry with you when you are sad.
> Cheer you on in your endeavors.
> Warn you when you start going the wrong way.

Our Evangel Christian High School had a home basketball game on Friday the twenty-seventh of January. Larry came to watch the game with me in our new gymnasium. Our team did not win, but it was fun to watch. After the basketball game, Larry and I went to Bob's Big Boy restaurant close to my home, where we ordered burgers and fries. We enjoyed talking to each other during our meal. Larry told me about his family. He was the youngest boy in his family. Larry's father died when Larry was just sixteen years old. His mother worked for the government and lived in an apartment close to Larry's. He had two older brothers. One of his sisters was older than him, and one was younger.

After dinner, as we were driving to my house, we had to stop at a red light. Larry took my hand and said, "You wear a size 7. I am going to get you a ring." Boy, was I shocked! Larry always seemed to come up with shocking statements. How did he know what size ring I wore? This guy was so earnest and sincere. This was just the third time we had gone out together. I did not know what to say. Things seemed to be moving too fast in this friendship.

When we arrived at my house, I invited Larry to a church social we were hosting at my parents' home the next Sunday night. He agreed to come. We said goodbye at my door. Larry placed his hand in the small of my back and held me close to his chest. As he embraced me, he gently laid his lips on mine and gave me a long memorable kiss that took my breath away.

I could not sleep that night. What was going on? I need time to think and pray. I had just told God in August I would be an "Old Maid" schoolteacher for Him. Here was this man, being so serious so quickly.

Dear Lord,

> I am unsure about what to do. I am mixed up. Please lead me in the paths You have prepared for me. Teach me daily to be more like Christ. Thank You for Larry's friendship. Show me what to do. I love You, Lord.

> > Your servant,
> > Terri

Amen.

Each path we face holds some unknown.
We ask for courage to take the first step.
It's hard to be out on your own.
But there is someone always with us—
Jesus.
He is strong and dependable.
We can face the future without fear.

Well, the next morning, I called my best friend, Shawne, and told her Larry was coming to the social the next Sunday night. I told her I had no idea how old he was, and I didn't know how to politely

MY SMART ROMANCE

ask him his age. He knew I was twenty-three because I had told him on our first date.

So we put our heads together and come up with a plan. Shawne was organizing games for our social. She would make one a "get acquainted" game where you had to fill out questions about yourself. Then Larry would fill in his age on the form. In that sneaky way, we could find out how old he was.

That Saturday night, my friends Shawne, Carol, Linda, and I went to a sacred concert in Washington, DC, at the DAR Constitution Hall. The concert was called "We Shall Behold Him." The music was outstanding at the Symphonic-Choral's presentation of worship and praise. To hear God's praises by a huge 250-voice choir was amazing. The hall rang with the glorious sound. It made me think of what it will be like in heaven when we are all singing God's praises. Tony Campolo was the speaker that night. As my friends and I rode home from DC, we were singing in the car the song "The Trees of the Field" from Isaiah 55:12 we had just heard at the concert.

The tune of that song reminded me of dancing to "Hava Nagila," an Israeli folk song, while in Israel. When I was a junior in college, I had the opportunity to go to Israel for six weeks. I went with a group called Baptist for Israel, led by Leland Crotts. Our group had a week of training in the United States before we flew to Israel. When we arrived in Tel Aviv, we were met with a big canvas-covered truck from the kibbutz. We rode on benches in the back of the truck packed so tight our knees touched the person sitting across from us. We swayed back and forth for over an hour in that hot truck.

I was finally deposited on Ashdot Ya'akov Ihud kibbutz with a dozen other volunteers. We were shown to our housing. I was assigned a little cement room with two other college-aged girl in our group. The room had three narrow cots and a window across from the door. Outside the room was a covered porch that ran the length of the long building, little cells opening off the porch. At the end of the porch was a utility sink (where I washed my cloths during my stay in Israel). The toilets and shower were located in another concrete building behind our sleeping accommodations.

Each day, as a volunteer, I was assigned a job. Some days I picked grapes. I cut bunches from the vines and placed them in a tray on a wheeled cart. Some days I cut banana flowers—a really messy job. The flowers dropped juice onto you that stained you and your clothes brown. I also washed dishes, worked in the laundry and in the plastic factory located on the kibbutz. I worked hard and learned how to do many different jobs. One day, my supervisor for the day laughingly said, "Too hot for dogs but not for volunteers" as he drove us out to work in the grapes.

A kibbutz is a communal type of living system. Everyone who lived on the kibbutz shared in the work and the profit. (But not volunteers. We worked for food and lodging only.) A central cafeteria cooked and fed the whole community. We ate three meals a day in that cafeteria. The only day we did not work was Shabbat or Sabbath. Saturday nights, we were assigned a family who lived on the kibbutz. We would visit our family and share food and stories with them.

The kibbutz took us on an outing one evening to swim in the Sea of Galilee. We rode from the kibbutz on a hay wagon behind a tractor. The tractor driver was wearing a Speedo. He kept guard over our group with an Uzi machine gun while we were at the beach. It made me feel very secure. The shore in the area we visited was really rocky. So it made me think, *Maybe that was why Jesus had to walk on the water.*

Our group did have times to tour and visit places in Israel during our stay. One weekend, we traveled to Jerusalem, and I saw the Wailing Wall, the Garden of Gethsemane, Golgotha, and the tomb where Jesus may have been buried. I missed the trip to Masada because I was sick that weekend. I spent the time in the bathhouse, hardly able to hold my head up.

That trip to Israel was a wonderful experience for me. It helped bring the Bible to life for me. I now pray for the peace of Jerusalem.

Larry called me right after Sunday morning church. He attended Maranatha Baptist Church, which was in Annandale, Virginia. His pastor was a young preacher named Wayne Fulton. Larry sang in the choir every Sunday. Larry has a wonderful tenor voice. He was so excited when he called me. He had preached at his church that morn-

MY SMART ROMANCE

ing, and he wanted to tell me about the experience. He really felt God wanted him to be a preacher someday.

After our Sunday Night worship at my church, we had a good crowd at the Sunday night social at my home. Most of the young teachers from the Christian school were there. Also, my pastor and his wife were present. Everyone was having a great time. We had some yummy snacks. One of the treats my mother made were "Nut Goodie Bars." Everyone was enjoying the good conversation and food.

Larry and I sat together on the piano bench. Pastor Gelina sat on the chair beside Larry, and Mrs. Gelina sat on the chair next to me. Shawne handed out the questionnaires she had prepared. Larry and I leaned our heads toward each other as we filled in the questions.

One question asked how old we were when we accepted Christ as our Savior. Well, I had been five years old when I was saved. My family lived in a duplex in New Jersey at that time. The house seemed huge to me! My family lived on the right half of the house, and the Greely family lived in the other half. In the basement, there was a little crack in the cement wall. I could see into the neighbors' basement. They had a ping-pong table in their basement.

The main floor of the house had a living room, a dining room, and a kitchen. A hall led right from the front door up to the steep stairs going to the second floor. Off to the right of that front hall was the door into the living room. The living room opened at the back right into the dining room. In the dining room, under the upstairs, was the door to go down to the basement. Through the dining room, you would go back to the kitchen. The back door out of the kitchen led onto a long-covered porch. The back porch ran the length of the duplex and was up in the air because in the back of the house, the basement was level with the ground. You could go right up to the neighbors' back door on that porch.

If you went up the front stairs to the third story, you came to the bedrooms and a bathroom. Then you could go up one more flight of stairs and be in the attic. There was a hole in the attic wall where you could peek into the lives of the neighbors also.

Our neighbors' family consisted of a mom, dad, and three children. All the children were older than me. The two sons I just ignored because they were boys. The younger boy was a twin with the only girl in their family. The daughter, Carol, had cerebral palsy. Her right side did not move smoothly. Her right hand turned in, kind of clawlike, and she dragged her right foot as she walked. She was lots of fun to play with. She always smiled and liked to do things with my little sister and me.

As we were out swinging under a big apple tree in our shared backyard, Carol asked me if I wanted to go to heaven. I had been going to Sunday school and church with my parents since I was five days old. I knew a lot about Jesus and the Bible. I said, "Well, sure I want to go to heaven!" Then Carol told me that the only way to get to heaven was to accept Jesus as my Savior. I needed to be saved from my sins. So right there, under that apple tree, I prayed and asked Jesus to save me so I could go to heaven.

I wanted my little sister; she was just three, to go to heaven too. So I told her she had to pray.

She crossed her arms at eye height on the apple tree. She leaned up against the tree and said jabber words. She did not really pray. I was very disappointed. She was too young to understand. She thought it was a game and just did what I told her to do.

I went into my side of the duplex and told my mother, "I just got saved!" I came to Jesus with the faith of a little child. I did not understand everything about the Bible, but I believed.

My mother was very pleased. However, she had a living room full of women from the church for some meeting. So she did not have time right then to ask me about my salvation. But she said, "That's great, dear! I will talk with you later about it." After the ladies left, Mom had time to sit down and hear about how I got saved.

At the party, Larry wrote that he had been saved when he was twelve years old. He wanted to ride the church bus, so he went to VBS, Vacation Bible School, just to ride the bus. His teacher at the Vacation Bible School led him to the Lord. He was attending Calvary Baptist Church in Washington, DC. Dr. Cloud was the pastor there. Dr. Cloud baptized Larry at Calvary Baptist soon after he was saved.

MY SMART ROMANCE

I found out that night, Larry was born May 19, 1947. I would never have guessed. He did not look like an old man. But Larry was twelve years older than I was! He was saved the year I was born. That was quite an age difference. But this age difference did not bother me too much. My grandparents on my father's side of the family had a difference of twenty years between Grandpa Ira and Grandma Lily. My father was ten years older than my mother. Age did not seem that important in the scheme of things to me.

I guess women in my family like older men, probably because older men are more mature.

Recipe for Nut Goodie Bars

Ingredients:

- 12 ounces chocolate chips
- 12 ounces butterscotch chips
- 1 cup creamy peanut butter
- 1 bag mini marshmallows
- 1 pound peanuts

Directions:

1. Grease 9×13 pan with butter.
2. Melt the two kinds of chips in a microwave-safe bowl in the microwave.
3. Add the peanut butter and mix.
4. Stir in the marshmallows and peanuts.
5. Press into the greased pan with buttered hands.
6. Cool, cut, and eat.

CHAPTER 5

Engagement

The first Friday in February, Larry took me to meet his older sister and brother-in-law. He wanted me to be acquainted with his family. I think Larry wanted to see if his family approved of me, or else he was showing me off. I was a little nervous about meeting his family. I had never been taken to meet any other boyfriend's family.

Dear Lord,

Help me not be too nervous and do something stupid to embarrass myself and Larry tonight.

Love,
Terri

Larry told me a little about his sister and brother-in-law. He was so glad that they both loved the Lord. He explained that this was a second marriage for both of them. We had to travel to their home in Maryland for dinner. Their house was a large colonial-style home. It had a wonderfully landscaped front yard. When I entered the front door, the house looked like it was straight out of a *Home Beautiful* magazine. I was taken into their formal living room, furnished with white couches and chairs. The windows were finished with beautiful boxed blue satin window covering. It was truly fancy. I was a little afraid to sit in such a beautiful place; I might get a spot on the furniture.

I was introduced to Larry's oldest sister, Joan, and her husband, Art Yow. Joan was a lovely blond, and Art looked a lot like Larry, with dark hair and the same type of mustache. Then a young girl came into the living room; she was Art's daughter, Denise. The whole family was happy Larry had found someone special in his life.

His sister seemed to be great at everything. Joan was a beautiful woman. She moved gracefully, like a ballerina. She worked as a secretary for a lawyer. She made porcelain dolls. She made and decorated beautiful cakes. Larry's sister was an excellent chef. She seemed like the perfect wife and mother. I felt a little intimidated by all that she could do. Would I be able to be a good a wife like Joan was?

She made us a delicious Mexican meal that night. It smelled spicy as we were seated around their formal dining room table to eat. Larry and I were seated on one side of the table. Art and Joan sat at each end of the table, and Denise sat across from Larry and I. Art led us in prayer before the meal. The food was terrific. Each mouthful was a pleasure. The salsa with the meal was excellent. It tasted just like the salsa served at Chi-Chi's restaurant. I asked if Joan made the salsa herself. She told me she had. I asked Larry's sister for the recipe. She replied, "Sorry, I do not give my recipe out to anyone." I felt a little hurt. I had never met anyone who did not share their recipes.

After the meal, I volunteered to do the dishes. Larry and I went to the kitchen. It was a marvelous place to work. We rolled up my sleeves and went to work. Larry helped me by drying the dishes as I washed them. We had fun working together in the kitchen. It was nice that Larry and I could work together so well.

Larry drove me around Washington, DC, on the beltway and back to my Virginia home. I laced my finger through Larry's so we could hold hands as he drove. Well, we held one hand as he used the other to steer the car. I could sit and watch Larry's handsome profile as he paid attention to his driving. He was so handsome. I enjoyed sitting close to him.

MY SMART ROMANCE

Larry asked what I thought of his sister and brother-in-law. I told him, "They seemed nice. They certainly have a beautiful home."

At my door, Larry hugged me. He put his hands in the center of my back and pulled me close with his arms encircling me. Then he kissed me tenderly. I loved having my head on his shoulder and hugging him. He smelled so good. I would breathe in deeply to savor his scent. When he got back to his apartment, he called me to say good night again and tell me he had enjoyed our night together.

February 3, I wrote in my journal this entry:

> I grew content in God's purpose for me. I am single by God's choice and can be happy that way. Thank You, God, for my being single.
>
> God has a plan in every chance meeting. And ours was no exception. God has a purpose and a Will in this situation.
>
> You are all I have longed for.
> There is nothing I could ask more.
> But my hesitation is real,
> For I want God's approval seal.

Saturday morning, Larry came to pick me up in his yellow Camaro. He wanted me to see his North Van Dorn Street apartment in Alexandria, Virginia. He lived in an apartment complex just off the main highway in Alexandria. The apartments were three stories tall. But Larry lived on the first floor. He had a private back patio entrance to his apartment, which made it feel more homelike.

When you entered through the patio door, you were right in the living room. The floor was covered with a deep red shag carpet. Larry even had a special rake to keep the carpet fluffy. He had a couch against the far wall. The couch was upholstered in a brown and golden Mediterranean motif and had a white and antique gold trimmed coffee table in front of it. Above the couch, Larry had hung a large painting of a boat on the water. The painting reminded Larry of Peter going fishing. Larry seemed very like Peter to me. He was a hardworking, direct-speaking man who loved Jesus.

To the right of the porch door was a big window with a dining table and four chairs in front of the window. The chairs were very modern. The backs were made of molded clear-brown plastic. The chair seats were white fake leather. The chairs swiveled around. A hall led to the kitchen on the right and bathroom on the left. The hall ended in a large bedroom with another window. Larry had a queen-size bed and a small dresser in his bedroom. His clothes were hung in a small closet off the bedroom. Everything was clean and orderly.

After the tour of his home, he took me for a walk in Fort Ward Park located next to his apartment complex. Fort Ward Park had Civil War canons mounted on raised fortifications of earth. The fort had been the Union defense for Washington, DC, against the Southern Army during the Civil War. The park had picnic and play areas scattered throughout its boundary.

Larry told me he once was riding his bike in this park and had an accident. The pedal fell off his bike, and he went head over handlebars. He cut his knee. And every time his heart would beat, blood shot out of his wound. A lady, who turned out to be a nurse, stopped her car to help him. She loaded him and his bike into her car. Larry sat in her car and held his leg together. The lady drove him to Alexandria Hospital, which was only a block away from the park. In the emergency room, the doctor stitched his knee back together. They also gave him a tetanus shot so he would not get lockjaw. That was how Larry got his scar on his knee.

That night, after visiting his apartment, Larry talked to my parents when I was out of the room. He was nervous. He said, "I would like to have your daughter's hand in marriage." He explained he had a good, secure government job. He was financially able to care for their daughter. He attended church faithfully every week. He loved the Lord and loved their daughter.

My parents had talked with Pastor McLean at their church previously. They had been curious about Larry. They wanted to know more about this guy dating their daughter. Pastor McLean had been Larry's pastor before retiring from the ministry at Calvary Baptist

Church. Larry had helped drive the church bus. He had served in *Awana*. Even though he was single, Larry had been elected a deacon of his church. Pastor McLean thought very highly of Larry.

My father and mother answered Larry's request for their daughter's hand by saying, "It is all right with us. But it is up to her to make her own decision."

I had some standards I wanted in the man I would consider marrying. First, he must be saved. Jesus needed to be his Savior. Then he must want to obey and serve Jesus. He must love God and His Word, the Bible. He needed to be faithful in church attendance and support of the church. Lastly, he must have a reliable job and be financially stable. Well, Larry checked all the right boxes. He was also very attractive and sang beautifully.

My mother wanted me to be sure I thought about my decision whether to marry Larry. She asked me some questions to make me think. First, she asked me, "Does the way he walks bother you?" She thought Larry walked like a duck. Well, his toes did turn sideways a little. But how he walked did not bother me.

Next, she wanted to know, "Does his stuttering bother you?" Well, Larry had stuttered all his life. He never wanted to go to grade school when little because he was afraid a teacher would call on him in class. He knew he could not answer any question without a long stutter. His mother used to follow him down the street from their low-income townhome in Washington, DC, to the school. She would use a little flexible branch she called a "keen switch" to switch his legs to make him go to school.

Larry had an inferiority complex because of his stuttering. He felt people look down on him and avoid him because of his stuttering. Larry could sing beautifully without stuttering. When Larry talked with me, he very seldom stuttered. He was more relaxed with me, and this reduced his stuttering. I hardly noticed his stuttering. I was not bothered that he had a speech impediment.

Mother also wanted to know how I felt about Larry's age. I explained to her that I was not bothered by that either. She knew age was not that important since she was ten years younger than my father. So my mother finally seemed satisfied that I had considered the things that she thought might be stumbling blocks to our relationship.

> Dear Lord,
>
> Give me wisdom in my decision about marriage. I want Your best for my life. Not my will but Yours be done.
> Amen.
>
> Your daughter,
> Terri

God answered my prayer and gave me peace about my decision. So when Larry asked me if I would marry him, I said, "Yes." February 5, 1984, I wrote in my journal.

> Lord, teach me to share my life.
> Teach me to understand and compromise.
> Lord, teach me to follow and obey.
> Under the head You place over me.
> Lord, make me a helper fit to my mate.
> Lord, help me learn to be patient and wait.

In my journal on February 7, I wrote,

> Warm, Secure, and Comfortable.
> That is how I feel in your arms.
> A haven for rest and encouragement.
> A place of fellowship and agreement.

Larry said he would wait to get married as long as I wanted. But in the very next breath, he said he would like to get married this summer.

Larry was so solemn. He was not a joker or jester. He took everything very seriously. When I met him, he only knew one joke.

MY SMART ROMANCE

Here it is: "What is a ghost mistake?" When you say, "I don't know?" he would say, "A boo, boo." I have a very sarcastic sense of humor. I liked comedies, but Larry did not. Larry did not always laugh at what I thought was funny.

The next Friday evening, February the 10, Larry was to take me to visit his mother. Before we left my house, Larry gave me my diamond engagement ring. He slid it on my ring finger on my left hand. It just fit because it was a size 7. It sparkled when the light hit it. I was so proud to wear his ring. I gave him a great big kiss.

Larry's mother, Evelyn, was a sweet Southern belle. She would say, with a strong Southern accent, "My daddy was the watermelon king of Bedford County, Virginia." When she was young, she would ride her pony down the long dirt driveway of her home to get the mail from the mailbox. She never drove or owned a car.

Larry's mother was shorter than I was. She wore her hair in a big blond hair-sprayed hairdo. She had a sweet smile and loving way about her.

She called Larry her "Buoy." He was her baby boy. Larry took her shopping at Safeway early every Saturday morning. He also picked her up and took her to church with him on Sunday mornings. Once when a roommate had deserted Evelyn, Larry even moved in with his mother to help her with the rent. She worked in a government office at the Pentagon. She rode the bus to get to work each day.

Evelyn gave Larry and me her blessings on our upcoming union. She was so pleased that Larry was engaged. He was the last of her five children to get married. Larry's two sisters and one brother had married while still teens. Larry had waited for me. If we had met when he was twenty, I would have only been eight years old, just a little girl.

When I was a little girl, about kindergarten age, I lived in Dwight, Illinois. My younger sister, Rhonda, and I were out playing in our yard. It was a chilly autumn day. We were a cute little pair, bundled in our warm coats, big red rubber galoshes, knit hats, and mittens. We jumped and ran around, but soon we were bored with those games. We wandered around and finally went into the garage.

While looking around, we found a small can of yellow paint. It was such a wonderful bright color. Yellow has always been my favorite color. But we had a problem: no brushes. You just cannot paint something without a brush. So two little girls put their heads together to solve the problem.

We found two old bottles of rubber cement. We knew each had a little brush in it to spread the sticky cement. We tried to open the bottle, but as the sticky stuff usually does, it had stuck the lids on the bottles. We finally figured it out. We slammed the bottles onto the concrete floor of the garage. We picked the brushes out of the shattered glass shards. Now we had our brushes to paint with.

Out of the garage, we went looking for what needed painting. The water pump in the yard looked like it could use some color. So we started there. We had lots of fun painting. We were not bored anymore.

Later, Mother came to find us and bring us into the house. What she found was not pleasing at all. There were two little girls with dabs and streaks of yellow paint on their winter coats, mittens, and boots. There was yellow paint on the pump, the cellar door, and the car. Fury and indignation rose quickly in Mother as she took in the scene.

Rhonda and I were marched into the house. We were washed and told, "Father will take care of this when he gets home." When we were really bad, Mom let Daddy talk to us and spank us when he came home from work.

It was a gloomy afternoon as we waited. Finally, Daddy came home. Mother spoke to him, and then he saw us. Sitting on the bed between us, he told us how disappointed and hurt he was that his little girls had been so bad. He told us we could have been hurt in all that broken glass. Daddy loved us and did not want his little girls hurt. He also explained we were renting this house, and it belonged to someone else. We were not to mess up other people's things.

After our talk, Daddy spanked us. Then all three of us sat on the bed and cried. Daddy's crying hurt more than the spanking. He loved us, and we had hurt him by our actions.

Our Father God is much like that. He loves us so much and wants our best. He doesn't want to see us hurt. But we do our own thing and endanger ourselves. Then He must clean up the mess we

MY SMART ROMANCE

have made and discipline us for our wrong actions. But He does not get pleasure from spanking us. It grieves Him that His beloved children have done something wrong.

Larry and I announced our engagement at our separate churches on Sunday, February 19, 1984. That was just about a month after we met.

When you are in the center of God's will things can happen fast. God's timing was just perfect—met in January, engaged in February, married in June?

Recipe for Joan's Salsa

Ingredients:

- 1 can tomatoes
- 1 small onion
- 1 green pepper
- 1 tablespoon lemon juice
- 1 teaspoon hot sauce
- 1 tablespoon vegetable oil
- 1 teaspoon salt
- 1 teaspoon oregano
- 1 jalapeño with seeds removed (or as many as you like). I have also used pickled jalapeños from a jar.

Directions:

1. Place all ingredients in blender.
2. Chop.
3. Chill.
4. Serve on any Mexican food or with tortilla chip.

Joan would not give this recipe to Terri. Later, after Larry and Terri were married, they went to the home of Larry's mom. Evelyn served them salsa and tortilla chips. Terri asked about the salsa. Evelyn said Joan had given her the recipe. Terri asked if she could have the recipe. Evelyn said sure. She gladly gave Terri a copy of the recipe. So now Terri gives the recipe away to anyone who asks for it. She even gives it to people who don't ask for it.

CHAPTER 6

Planning for a Wedding

Well, we were engaged. Larry wanted to get married this summer. How?

I got a little book about planning a wedding with a checklist by the editors of *Brides* magazine. The first sentence of the booklet said, "A formal wedding takes a minimum of six months to arrange properly." So we counted up, and June was only four months away. Boy, we had a lot of catching up to do so we could have our formal wedding.

> Dear Lord,
>
> Please direct us as we make plans for our wedding.
> Amen.

First, we had to pick a date. Well, my parents' twenty-sixth wedding anniversary was coming up on Saturday, June 23. God had been good to them. They had a happy, Christ-honoring marriage. So Larry and I thought that June 23 would be a good day for our wedding. We could share our wedding anniversary with my parents. So at least we had a date chosen for the wedding.

We went out to dinner on Valentine's Day to the SeaGalley. The building had a rowboat on the roof, so you could tell it was a seafood restaurant. I ordered fried clams, and Larry had fish and chips.

While we dined, we discussed our plans for the wedding. We would be married at my church, Evangel Baptist Church, in Dale City, Virginia. We would have the reception in the church gym/ fellowship hall called Martin Hall. We would each make up an invitation list for our family members to be invited. We would also invite both our churches and all the students and parents from the Christian school I taught at. So this would be a large wedding. My pastor, Richard Gelina, would be officiate for our wedding. Also, Larry's dear friend, Pastor McLean, would give a charge to the bride and groom. We got a lot of our planning out of the way that Valentine's Day. We were so excited about our plans.

Our planner said to "choose attendants six months before the wedding." I wanted to have two bridesmaids: I wanted Shawn, my best friend and fellow teacher, to be an attendant. I also wanted Faye, my freshman roommate and friend as the other attendant. My sister, Rhonda, was to be my maid of honor. So I quickly contacted all three and arranged for them to be my attendants. Shawne lived with her parents in Dale City, so she was close. Faye lived in Ohio with her husband, Kurt. (I had been a bridesmaid at their wedding.) My sister, Rhonda, lived in Minnesota. They all agreed to be at my wedding.

The planner said, "Three months before the wedding, order attendants' dresses." I am very practical and economical. I wanted the bridesmaid dresses to be usable as Sunday dresses after the wedding. I did not want my three attendants to have bridesmaid dresses they could never wear again. Prairie-style dresses were in fashion at that time. So I chose a country pattern that I really liked. The dress was high necked with a little white lace around the neck. The bodice had a V of ruffles from shoulder to the middle of the chest, also bordered by lace. The sleeves were elbow length with a ruffle. The skirts had a ruffle that ended a little below the knee. Then I chose three colors of the same cotton print. Rhonda would have a violet dress. Shawn would get a light blue dress. Faye's dress would be pink. My mother is a wonderful seamstress. When I was young, I gave my

MY SMART ROMANCE

mother a trophy for Mother's Day. I made the trophy all by myself. I stuck a needle in a Styrofoam thread spool, then I spray-painted it gold. On the golden trophy, I put a little card that said, "To the Best Sewer," because she could sew so well. My mother still laughs when she looks at her trophy on the shelf in her room.

My mother sewed all three dresses for my bridesmaids. They turned out beautifully. We gave the dresses as gifts to my bridesmaids. My mother was such a big help in preparing for my wedding.

The wedding planner recommended at three months, "Order flowers that match wedding color scheme." My mother and I decided we would have silk flowers at the wedding. Live flowers smell nice and look lovely, but they do not last very long. One of the ladies at our church volunteered to arrange all the flowers. So all we had to do was buy the silk flowers. I loved a rainbow of colors. The flowers for my wedding reflected that love. So my mother and I purchased violet, blue, pink, yellow, and white flowers.

I wanted the bridesmaids to carry baskets of flowers. The ribbons tied to the basket handles matched the color of each bridesmaid's dress. I thought that after the wedding, the basket could be used as a table decoration by my bridesmaids. My bouquet had blue morning glories, pink flowers, yellow daisies, and white roses. It was fashioned with a swag hanging down about two feet from a circle of flowers. My bouquet had ribbons hanging with the flowers in all the colors used in the bridesmaids' baskets.

Larry chose three men to stand up with him. His best man was his brother-in-law, Art Yow. He also asked two friends from church, Wayne Naylor and John Hall, to be his groom's men. Larry went to the men's formal shop and looked at what was available. He decided on gray tuxedos with lighter pearl gray vest and gray ties for the groomsmen and himself. The men would wear white shirts and dark gray tuxedo trousers. My father also ordered a tuxedo to wear to the wedding to match the groom and his groomsmen.

The planner book said, "Visit the clergy with your fiancé six months before the wedding." So we talked to Pastor Gelina about officiating our wedding on Wednesday, February 29 (1984 was a leap year), only four months before the wedding. He was available on our planned wedding day, which seemed like a good sign we had chosen a great date for the wedding. Pastor Gelina agreed to marry us and set up times for Larry and me to meet with him for premarital counseling.

On April 23, two months before the wedding, I found my wedding dress. I went to the Springfield Mall, the closest mall to my house. In a store called David's Village Shop, I found the dress for me. It was a white "Romantic Renaissance Bridal Collection" dress in white cotton. It was a Gunne Sax creation designed by Jessica McClintock. It had a high neck with lace, elbow-length sleeves with lace ruffles, a layered, ruffled skirt with the back split with ruffles running up each side to meet at the waist in the middle of dress's back.

The waist was accented with a satin belt that tied in a bow at my back. I thought this dress went along with the bridesmaids' dresses wonderfully. It matched my prairie theme.

Larry said I could choose the invitations for our wedding. So I looked through books and books of different kinds of wedding invitations at the printers. I never knew there were so many different invitations. I finally decided on one trifold card on ivory stock. A pearlized picture of pink roses held the flaps closed in the front center of the card. After choosing the card, I had to decide what to say inside the invitation. I read through lots of wordings for wedding invitations. I never knew there were so many ways to invite people to a wedding. I worked on the wording for a couple of days, finally putting a couple of different invitations together, I got what I wanted. This is what I finally decided on:

Because you have shared in their lives
by your friendship and love
you are invited to join with us as
Terri Lynn and Mr. Larry Ray Packard
exchange marriage vows and unite in Christ
on Saturday, the twenty-third of June
nineteen hundred and eighty-four
at ten thirty o'clock in the morning

MY SMART ROMANCE

at Evangel Baptist Church
of Dale City, Virginia
You are invited to celebrate their union
at a reception immediately following
in Martin Hall
If you are unable to attend, we ask
your presence in thought and prayer
Mr. and Mrs. Ira Smart

The invitations arrived from the printers early enough to be addressed and sent on time. Larry and I had finally finished making our guest lists. My mother and I addressed all the invitations. There were hundreds of them. Then we mailed them out right on time one month before the wedding day. My tongue was sore from licking all those envelopes, not from kissing Larry.

At six months, the planner recommended, "Plan the reception." A friend of my mother from church, Eva Aikin, volunteered her time to help make the reception buffet meal. Eva had catered for other events and knew how to cook for a large crowd. My family just had to purchase all the ingredients. My favorite sandwich of all time was a tuna fish salad sandwich. So for the reception I wanted tuna fish salad sandwiches. My mom bought a case of canned tuna fish to make enough salad for a crowd. We also would have big punch bowls full of potato salad. A watermelon would be cut to look like a basket and be used as a serving bowl filled with fruit salad. We planned for bowls full of strawberries and platters of raw vegetables. We ordered fresh rolls from our local grocery store bakery to be ready early the day of the wedding. We would have punch, water, and coffee to drink. The reception refreshments were all planned.

My students volunteered to decorate the reception hall the week of the wedding. They would put up bunting and signs they had made all around the gym. They would help make a lollipop tree with lollipops hung by yarn on a large branch set up in a pot of sand. A pair of scissors was on the tree, so the children could cut a lollipop off the tree. There was to be a white garden archway hung with paper wedding bells in the middle of the hall. Tables would be set up all around the gym with white tablecloths.

A wedding cake was also on our wedding checklist. I went to a cake decorator's home and tasted her different cakes with my mother. We decided on a three-tier cake that would serve three hundred guests. The base was made of two big round layers. Each layer had two cakes in it: one vanilla and one chocolate. The sides of each layer would have scallops of white frosting and cascades of frosting flowers. Beautiful blue morning glories and colorful frosting flowers would enhance each cascade. In the center of the first layer would be a small basket with flowers and ribbons, matching the bridesmaids' baskets. Columns held up the second layer. The middle layer was graced by a pair of porcelain swans in the center. Columns held up the top layer, to be saved for our first anniversary.

My mother found the perfect cake topper. It was a bride-and-groom music box that played Mendelssohn's "Wedding March." The bride on the topper had brown hair like mine. The dress on the porcelain bride looked a lot like my wedding dress. My mother painted a brown mustache on the groom figure so he would look like Larry. That made the cake topper just perfect for Larry and my wedding.

We found a photographer we could afford. He would take pictures during the ceremony. Then after the ceremony, he would take posed pictures of us with our attendants and families. Also, a man from my church, who worked at a film-developing plant, offered to develop for free any photos we had of the wedding. So we bought a bunch of disposable cameras for people to use at the wedding and reception.

I wanted Larry to sing to me at our wedding. I loved to hear him sing. His sweet tenor voice just thrills me. The song we chose for Larry to sing was "I Could Never Promise You" by Don Francisco. He practiced the song with my sister's best friend, Lori Fisher, playing the piano. We also asked Carol Kersey to play the piano prelude before the wedding service. Debbie Hanel agreed to play the organ for the wedding march on our special day.

The planning for the formal wedding seemed to be coming together nicely, even if we did it all in just four months.

MY SMART ROMANCE

Recipe for Tuna Salad

Ingredients:

- 1 can tuna fish, drained
- 2 tablespoons Miracle Whip
- 1 chopped-up dill pickle
- 1/2 cup chopped onion

Directions:

1. Put all ingredients in a bowl.
2. Mix well.
3. Serve on bread, crackers, or lettuces.

CHAPTER 7

Cards and More Cards

One of the reasons Larry and I got to know each other so well during our short four-month courtship was the cards. Larry really liked the card selection at the Washington Bible College bookstore, where he was going to school. Every time he went to a night class, he would buy me cards. Larry chose the cards for their lovely pictures and romantic sentiments inside. Then he would write little sweet notes on the cards and mail them to me.

For Valentine's Day, he sent me two cards that arrived a day apart. One of the cards was pink with flowers that said:

Beloved, let us love one another. I John 4:7

On this special day of love, I'm sending this Valentine just to say, God has given you the gift of sharing His love in a special way!

Inside the card, he wrote this personal note:

Dear Terri,

Thank you for coming into my life. God has given to us a relationship that can grow, just

as our one with the Lord. I love you very much.
You have made me very happy.

Love,

Larry XX

2 Peter 3:18 "But grow in grace, and in the
knowledge of our Lord and Savior, Jesus Christ."
May our prayer be to grow in Him, together.

I wrote Larry a card or letter every time I received one in the mail
from him. I sent him a Precious Moments card with this inscription:

Love is a song that's so sublime
when you're the theme Dear Valentine.

Inside I wrote this to Larry:

John 13:34–35 "A new commandment I
give unto you. That ye love one another; as I have
loved you, that ye also love one another. By this
shall all men know that ye are my disciples, if ye
have love one to another." I LOVE YOU!

With all my love forever, Terri XO

The beginning of March, I sent Larry a card with lily of the
valley flowers on it and the verses 1 Corinthian 13:4–7. Inside I wrote
to Larry:

To My love,

Each time we are together, I learn more
about the man I am going to spend the rest of my
life with. That is very good! So I will know how

to act and react. When we are married, we will not be surprised (so much) about each other.

I am praying daily for you. God has great things planned for you. I want to be an encouragement and help in any area of my life that I can. God will be with us as we read His Word, pray, and share our faith with others.

Today I counseled two girls at school. There is bitterness between them. We read Luke 17:3–10 and looked at what forgiveness really is. Forgiveness is a Promise. You promise three things: 1. Not to bring up the offense to the person; 2. Not to bring it up to others; 3. Not to stew about it. The girls asked each other for forgiveness. We prayed together. I am going to check up on them.

I love you very much! I miss being with you!

All my love, Terri

Larry sent me a card that said "God Bless You" on the outside. Inside it said, "Just sending this card to let you know how very special you are to me."

Larry penned this message inside the card:

Dear Terri,

Thank you for your thoughtful letter today. I really look forward to reading them. They let me know what you're doing when I'm not with you. I too miss you when we are not together. My prayers and thoughts are with you every day when you are teaching. The Lord will use you as you are faithful to Him. The Lord is so good to us. Praise His name forever with me!

I love you very much. I like to see you smile at me. You have a beautiful smile. Thank you for that. Thank you that you have a love for God's Word as I do! Psalm 71, "In you, O Lord, I put my trust..."

Love always,
Larry XX

(If you do not know, X's stand for kisses. O's stand for hugs.)

Sometimes Larry wrote me letters on notebook paper while waiting for his evening class. One letter I received said:

Dearest Terri,

Thank you for a beautiful weekend together. I had a nice time with you and your mom and dad.

It was fun playing card games together as a family.

I've been reading getting ready for class tonight, and I thought that I'd write this letter to share with you. I Love you very much. Love occupies a great portion of God's Word. Love is at the heart of salvation (John 3:16); Love is the first named fruit of the Spirit (Galatians 5:22–23); Love is the motivation for obedience to the mandates of our Lord (John 15:15; 2 Cor. 5:14).

One of the evidences of love is the complimentary attitude of those in love toward each other. Those who truly love each other should feel no embarrassment in voicing their feelings for each other.

To express love in word and deed is to show strength, not weakness.

Honey! I am looking forward to spending the rest of my life with you. There are many things we can do together to honor our Lord Jesus Christ. May we always do God's will and live for Him and His glory.

Love,
Larry XX

I answered his letter right away with one of my own.

Dearest Larry,

I could hardly believe your letter got here so fast! I received it today, and you were just writing it yesterday! Our mail service is pretty good here in Virginia. To send a letter from Ohio to Virginia, it took at least 5 days. Sometimes I think the mail comes via a slow boat from China. But I have nothing to complain about getting a letter in less than 24 hours!

I miss you a lot. Last night I felt like something was missing because I didn't talk to you. Mom told me this morning that you called. Sorry I wasn't up to talk to you. Talking makes my day!

I gave three tests today. I have papers to grade in all my classes. I will just have to sit down and put my mind to getting them all graded.

Softball practice is to begin March 12. I have practice every day, except Wed. The girls are already signing up. We can't get a field till March 31, so we will start practice in our parking lot and on rainy days in our gym.

MY SMART ROMANCE

The flowers you gave me this weekend are lovely. They smell wonderful also. When I look at them, I think of what a great guy I am getting for a husband.

My future is such a bright time for me now. I look forward to each new day. I can see God working each day to make me the person I need to be for Him. God's will is what I am trying to follow. As He leads us closer together, I see this as a way God will help us each grow as His children.

I want us to build a God-centered home, based on God's Word, supported by prayer. I want us to stand with Joshua and be able to say with him, "As for me and my house, we will serve the Lord." Josh. 24:15

I love you very much. Each day my love grows deeper. I promise to love you all my life. I also want God's love to flow through me to you all my life.

Always yours,
Terri

Larry sent me a card with a picture of a couple beside a waterfall. It said on the outside, "All the world is beautiful when seen through eyes of love."

The inside the card was printed:

I never knew how wonderful life could be...
how beautiful love could be...
until you came into my world.

TERRI LYNN SMART PACKARD

Larry wrote to me:

Sweetie,

I love you very much and think of you, wondering what you are doing when I'm not with you. God says that the Pathway of truth and love is to walk in the truth of God's Word and Jesus Christ and to love one another, and this is love, that we walk after His commandments. II John 4–6

When I think of you, it makes my day a little brighter. I look forward to being with you and to doing things together. May God Bless you as you seek to do His will.

I Love you!!

Larry XX

I sent Larry a Ziggy card that had this sentiment on it:

You're a born leader… I'd follow you anywhere!

Here is my note to him:

To My Dearest,

I love you. Only 39 days left. I am looking forward with anticipation to our wedding day.

I am glad your exam is over. I know you did your best. I am glad we studied the material together this past weekend. I learned a lot from the study.

MY SMART ROMANCE

You are my sweetheart. I love you very much. I want to be with you always. Like the card says, 'I'd follow you anywhere.'

God is so good to us. We must always be thankful for His love and care for us. I love you!

Terri

In May, we celebrated Larry's birthday. Larry and I went to the high school sport's banquet the night of his birthday. I made him a "Strawberry Jell-O Cake." I included some gift cards with his birthday presents. One card said:

Happy Birthday to the Best Guy in the World! I hope this is a great year for you. It has been already for me. I love you! Let's get married!!

In the other card I wrote:

Happy Birthday! I love you very much!! You are the person God planned especially for me!! I hope you have an enjoyable birthday and we can celebrate lots and lots more as the years together go by!!

Love Terri.
(I know I must be in love. Look at all the exclamation marks I used.)

Larry sent me a card with flowers on it that said, "With loving thoughts…because you're special." He wrote inside the card:

Dearest Terri,

Thanks for the nice weekend we had together. It was fun playing games together with

63

your parents. I love you very much. Thanks too for the nice gifts for my birthday. It was the best birthday because we are together.

This verse from Isaiah 40 came to my mind the other day. "God will renew our strength. Have you not known? Have you not heard? The everlasting God, the Lord. The Creator of the ends of the earth. Neither faints nor is weary. There is no searching of His understanding. He gives power to the weak, and to those who have no might He increases strength. But those who wait on the Lord shall renew their strength." Thank you for Loving me!

Love Always,
Larry XX

When I get a letter
It brightens the whole day.
I feel so much better
As I travel my way.
So send me a letter
I will write back today.

Every weekend, Larry and I spent time doing things together. We would go out to dinner or eat with my parents. We went bowling, played ping-pong, went shopping, and had picnics. We attended a Prince Williams Pirates single-A baseball game. We got to see Barry Bonds play once before he became famous. Larry really likes baseball. We visited his sister and brother-in-law in Maryland a few times. Sometimes we would play Atari in my parents' basement. I was not very good at the video games. After playing Atari, we would cuddle and kiss. That made it more fun.

On Sundays, we sometimes attended his evening church services at Maranatha Baptist Church and sometimes attended my evening church service at Evangel Baptist Church together. Then Larry would come over to my house after the evening services. We loved spending time together. But I had to teach school Monday mornings, so sometimes I would have to tell him to go home so I could get enough sleep to be ready for work Monday.

Larry was always looking for lovely gifts to give to me. Larry gave me a pearl necklace. Later he gave me pearl earrings. He gave me a heart necklace and a mug. He gave me a beautiful Hallmark heart wall plaque with a sweet sentiment.

> To the One I Love
> There are joys two hearts, and only two can share...
> The joys that love, and only love, can give.

He was always showering me with flowers. Love can only be known by the actions it prompts. One of the ways Larry showed his love for me was with all those gifts.

Dear Father,

> Thank You for lettering me get to know Larry through his letters. Lead us in the path You have for us. May we be Your servants.
> Amen.

I was so in love. Like one of the cards I wrote to Larry said, "I wanted to kiss his face off."

Recipe for Strawberry Jell-O Cake

Ingredients:

- 1 box white cake mix and required eggs, oil, and water per box instructions
- 1 box of Jell-O (I like strawberry but any flavor will do.)
- 1 carton whipped topping
- Fresh or canned fruit to match the Jell-O flavor

Directions:

1. Make the cake in a 9×13 pan as directed by the box instructions.
2. When baked, cool for five minutes.
3. While cake is cooling, make the Jell-O according to the directions.
4. Poke holes all over the cake with a fork.
5. Pour the Jell-O over the cake. Refrigerate till the Jell-O is set up.
6. Frost the cake with the whipped topping, and decorate with the fruit.
7. Keep refrigerated till served.

CHAPTER 8

Cooking

Larry turned to me one night, right after I had my diamond ring, and said, "We are engaged now, and I don't even know if you can cook." What would he do if I could not cook? Would he ask for his ring back?

Well, I told him I did know how to cook. I would cook dinner for him to prove it. So we set up a dinner date for Friday, February 17. I knew just what I would cook for him. I really enjoy Oriental food, and one of my favorite dishes is "Pepper Steak" with rice. That was what I planned to make.

Food is an important part of friendship. Sharing a meal together gives you time to get to know a person better. Cooking food for someone can be very intimate. You put love in everything you make.

That is why my grandmother always said, "Eat some more!"

That Friday, at school, I was the chapel speaker. We had chapel once a week. The teachers took turns speaking. I talked about the "I Ams" of Jesus in the book of John. In the Old Testament, God told Moses at the burning bush to tell the people, "I Am that I Am." Jesus was God and used the I *Am*s to describe Himself.

In John 6:35, Jesus said, "I *Am* the Bread of Life." Christ provides spiritual food so we do not need to hunger or thirst. In John 8:12, Jesus said, "I *Am* the Light of the World." Believers do not need to walk in darkness but in the Light from God's Word. Jesus said in John 10:7, "I *Am* the Door." We can enter into new life in Christ.

Then in John 10:11 and 14, Jesus said, "I *Am* the Good Shepherd." Jesus the good shepherd gave His life for the sheep. Jesus told Martha in John 11:25, "I *Am* the Resurrection and the Life." Believe in Jesus, and you will have eternal life and never die. Jesus said in John 14:6, "I *Am* the Way, the Truth, and the Life." There is only one way to the Father: through Jesus Christ. In John 15:1, Jesus described Himself by saying, "I *Am* the Vine." Without Jesus, we can do nothing. We must stay connected to Him to live and grow for the Lord.

The chapel service went really well. The students paid attention. I prayed they learned that Jesus was the only way of salvation. Jesus would prepare a place in heaven for them if they accepted Him as their Savior.

When I got home from school that Friday, I started cooking. The preparation was not too difficult for my planned meal. There were things that needed chopped up. The beefsteak had to be sliced thinly. The onions and green peppers must be julienne cut. I got out my mom's electric skillet. I started browning the meat, onion, and garlic. The house took on a lovely aroma. I started the long grain rice at just the right time. Everything would be ready at the same time for our meal. That can be the hard part about cooking: getting everything ready at the same time.

I set the large dining room table for two. My parents graciously gave me the use of the house for the meal that night. Larry and I would be dining alone. The table was a long one, with a captain's chair and a mate's chair on each end. There were benches for seats on each side of the table. I set our dinner places right beside each other, not way apart on the ends of the table. That way, we could sit close to each other. I liked to be close to Larry.

I used the best china. I placed a folded napkin beside each plate, a knife and spoon on the napkin to the right of the plates, and a fork on the left of the plate. The salad plates were above the dinner plates. Crystal goblets were set in place to receive our drinks. Everything looked inviting on the table.

As I cooked, I thought about my future husband. The muscles of his upper arm were so firm and solid. I could feel his strength as I wrapped my arms around them. They were so attractive to me;

they made me feel safe. I could envision his broad shoulders, trim waist, and flat backside. Larry was always so clean and neat, dressed so debonair. His eyes are so blue, and at times there was the cutest twinkle in them.

I hurried down to my room to get dressed up before Larry arrived. I wanted to look attractive to him. I brushed my hair and thought of Larry's smile. I put on a favorite dress because I knew Larry liked it. I touched on a little makeup and a splash of perfume. I did not use any lipstick or lip gloss. Larry did not like to kiss it, and I wanted to get a few kisses. I was looking forward to our evening together.

Dear Father,

May our daily bread not be as important to us as feeding on your Word.
In Jesus's name,
Amen.

The meat in the "Pepper Steak" was tender and flavored just right. The white rice was fluffy and not stuck together. We had green beans and a salad, with Italian dressing as our side dishes. Fresh rolls and butter added to our enjoyment of our meal. Finally, we had brownies for dessert. The chocolate, full of endorphins, made us smile. Larry really enjoyed the whole meal. He even had seconds. I enjoyed making the food that would please Him. Larry now knew I could cook.

When dinner was over, we worked together to clear off the table. We did the dishes together. I washed, and Larry dried. Then I challenged Larry, "Well, I cooked for you. How about you cooking for me? How do I know if you can cook?"

Larry took up the challenge, inviting me to his apartment the next weekend to sample his cuisine. Larry did not usually cook. He ate out a lot of the time at local restaurants. In those days, Larry could eat out cheap. The *blue-plate special*, where Larry went, would cost him only $1.99. Larry did know how to make the quick instant rice that you just place the plastic package into boiling water. After the allotted time, you take the bag out of the water and put the rice on your plate. But that was about the extent of his culinary ability at that time.

He planned a menu he thought would be romantic. He wanted to make "Stuffed Jumbo Shells" in marinara. He loved Italian food. But how was he to make it? He found a good recipe and made a shopping list.

Larry went to the local grocery store for the ingredients he would need. All that was available in his refrigerator were half-empty glass bottles of Pepsi. After shopping, he called his older sister, Joan, for tips on how to make the jumbo shells. He found out how to boil the pasta. He mixed the cheeses to fill the shells. He even made a meat and tomato sauce from scratch. He browned the hamburger with onions, green peppers, and spices. Larry added the tomatoes and simmered his sauce for a long time.

He went out of his way to make it special. It took him the whole day to prepare and cook.

When I arrived at his apartment that evening the room was darkened, with candles glowing on the table. The aroma of oregano and basil filled the whole apartment. On the table was a bouquet of pink carnations Larry had purchased just for me. Everything about his dinner looked so lovely.

Larry pulled out my chair and sat me at the table, touching my arm tenderly as he helped me.

His touch sent a thrill from my arm all over my body. How could his touch be so electric? Larry's touch sent chills through me that made me feel warm.

Larry sat down in the other chair and took both my hands in his and prayed. He thanked the Lord for our time together and for our meal. After prayer, Larry brought to the table his Corelle plates. Each plate held one jumbo pasta shell, filled with creamy cheese and covered in a remarkable crimson sauce. I had never had jumbo shells before. I cut my shell and placed the warm pasta in my mouth.

The rich, spicy tomato sauce and the creamy cheese blended on my taste buds. It tasted wonderful. I cleaned my plate. His main dish was a brilliant success.

Larry had focused so much on making his main dish; he did not consider having any side dishes or a dessert. So we settled for hugs and kisses by candlelight for dessert.

They say the way to a man's heart is through his stomach. But I had won Larry's heart before he even tasted my cooking. Well, we found out we both could cook. But I would be the main chef in our future home.

Recipe for Pepper Steak and Rice

Ingredients:

- 1 pound beef, sliced
- 1 onion, sliced
- 1 clove garlic, minced
- 1 green pepper, sliced
- 1 tablespoon vegetable oil
- 2 tablespoons soy sauce
- 1 teaspoon black pepper
- 2 cups water
- 1 tablespoon cornstarch, mixed in 1/4 cup cold water

Directions:

1. Brown the beef with the onions and garlic in vegetable oil in electric skillet.
2. Add the soy sauce, black pepper, and water. Deglaze the skillet.
3. Cover and simmer till beef is tender. Add more water as needed. Do not let it go dry.
4. Add the green peppers, and steam with the lid on for 10 minutes.
5. If needed, add more water so you can have gravy on the meat. Bring to a boil.
6. Stir in the cornstarch mixture. Boil for 1 minute. This should thicken the juice to a nice brown gravy.
7. Serve over steamed rice.

How to make steamed rice:

Ingredients:

- 1 cup rice
- 2 cups water

MY SMART ROMANCE

Directions:

1. Put water and rice in a medium-sized pan.
2. Bring to a boil. Stir once.
3. Cover and reduce heat to simmer.
4. Cook for 20 minutes.
5. Uncover and fluff. (If the rice is still too wet, cook a few more minutes.)

CHAPTER 9

Spring and Easter

Larry and I were very busy. I was teaching school every weekday. He was working and going to night college classes. Our churches had functions we attended together most weekends. We went out to dinner together. We spent as much time as we could together. We felt like we were in a whirlwind of activity, but it was great.

We went to two sweetheart banquets that February. One was a church event. The second banquet was for Evangel Christian High School. I was a chaperon at the function. Larry and I dressed up formally for these special occasions. Larry was so handsome in his dark suit and colorful ties. I wore long fancy dresses. My students liked to see their teacher with a fella. They would giggle about us and talk behind our backs about our romance. We got our picture taken together the night of the school's valentine banquet with a heart behind us on the bulletin board that had our names in the center with a pulse sign between them. It was just like what teenagers write in the margin of their notebooks.

At school events, there was no PDA. PDA stood for public display of affection. Another term used for that was "making purple." Girls were pink, and boys were blue. And if you mixed those colors, you were "making purple." So we did not hold hands or kiss where the students could see us. But when Larry and I were alone, we enjoyed holding hands and sharing hugs and kisses. We kept from temptation by being in well-lit places and not all alone. Usually, Larry came to

MY SMART ROMANCE

my house, and my parents were in the house with us, so we were chaperoned.

I had to organize and oversee the school's science fair that spring. Everyone in my science classes had to work on a science fair project. First, they had to come up with an idea. Then they had to research and write a paper. Next, they had to do an experiment and collect data. The last thing the students had to do was set up a display to show all their hard work. Well, as the teacher, I had to read all those reports and grade all those projects. I had to advise on their experiments. Then at the time of the fair, I had to get judges willing to look at all those displays. The science fair was set up on tables in the fellowship hall at the school so everyone could see the students' hard work.

The very next week, I served as a judge for Engleside Christian School's Science Fair in Alexandria, Virginia. That was the school where I attended and graduated high school. I started going to Engleside Christian School in the ninth grade as a high school freshman. My mother stated working at a Calvary Baptist School as a kindergarten teacher, so my family could afford the tuition at Engleside for my sister and me.

When I attended Godwin Middle School in the eighth grade, I did not want to be different from the other students. But my classmates called me Grandma because my dresses were to my knees and not miniskirts. So I told my parents when I got Cs "Cs are an average grade, and I am an average student." I did not really try in most of my classes. The only place I really excelled was in science and band. I played the bassoon, but I did not practice enough.

When I started high school, my mother and father were sacrificing so I could attend this private Christian school. So I put my mind to my studies. I did my homework. I studied for tests, even the spelling ones that I hated. Mr. Stallard was one of my favorite high school teachers. His twins, Vance and Jolene, were in my class. Mr. Stallard taught my Bible classes, and he taught me beginning Greek. When I was a senior in high school, I took consumer math with Mr. Stallard. He allowed me to teach the class because I was ahead in math. Then four years after I started at Engleside Christian School,

I graduated at the top of my class with straight As. I was the school's valedictorian in 1978. On graduation day, I wore a long, white dress under my white cap and gown. I delivered my valedictorian speech to my class and all the audience that day.

I thanked my parents for all they had done for me. I also challenged my class to live for Jesus.

Now here I was, the teacher at a Christian school, and I had lessons to prepare in six different classes. On Monday mornings, I had to turn in my lesson plans for the classes to the principal. I gave daily notes, and usually I had handouts for each class that had to be manufactured. Next, there were quizzes and tests to make up. Then I had to grade everything and record the grades in my grade book.

Dear Lord,

Help me find the time to do my job to the best of my ability for You. Give me wisdom. I don't always know what to do or say.

Love,
Your child, Terri

One of the hardest parts of my job teaching was the parent-teacher conferences. I had to sit at a table in the fellowship hall of the church one whole evening. The parents would come and sit with me at the table. I had to explain how their student was performing in my class. Most parents thought their student could do no wrong. So if I had to tell them their student was not doing well, I had to be prepared to defend my decision for giving them the grade they deserved. I also had to discuss with the parents the behavior problems their student had in my class.

I was offered a contract at Evangel Christian School to work the next school year. I did some serious praying and thinking about it. Should I sign and teach next year or not sign? Larry could take care of me financially. I would not need to work as his wife, but I had only known Larry a few months. What if something made us break up and not get married? How would I support myself then? I discussed it with Larry, and he was fine with whatever I decided about the job. Finally, I had peace from the Lord and signed the contract. I was going to work the next school year my first year of marriage, I hoped.

Larry and I went to "Singspirations" together that spring. Both of us loved to sing God's praises.

We had a wonderful time on those dates as we sang hymns, psalms, and spiritual songs. Spending a whole two hours lifting our voices to exclaim how great our God is was exhilarating.

Larry had sung since he was a little boy. As a boy in Washington, DC, he would sing Elvis Presley songs for money on the street corners. He sounded just like Elvis when he sang songs like "I'm All Shook Up," "Don't Step On My Blue Suede Shoes," and "Love Me Tender." He would use the money he got for singing to go to the movies.

During spring in Virginia, the flowers are swaying in the breeze, purple crocus, red tulips, and yellow daffodil colors all around. The red bud trees display their beautiful maroon buds against their dark, almost black, bark. The dogwood trees unfold their flowers of four white petals to remind us of Christ's crucifixion. The dark mark at the top petal is for the blood from Christ's crown of thorns. A mark on each side petal stands for the nail-pierced hands. A spot at the bottom show that Christ's feet were nailed to the cross. That spring, Easter was a special time, remembering Christ is Risen. He is Alive! He died for my sins. Then Jesus came back alive after three days.

I always got new clothes for Easter. I usually picked out a pair of shoes and a matching purse for Easter Sunday. When I was little, I always had a hat and white gloves to finish my Easter outfit. My mom and I usually had to sew my dresses in the eighties. I wanted to have the hem of my dresses below my knees. The fashion at that time was for short skirts and bare midriffs. Those were not very modest. So I sewed myself a new dress for Easter that spring.

Plans were made for an Easter lunch at Joan and Art's home. We would bring Larry's mother, Evelyn, with us when we went to Maryland from Virginia after the Easter Sunday morning service.

Maranatha Baptist Church was having an outdoor sunrise service on Easter morning. Larry and I decided to attend that special service. But Larry's mother did not want to go to the church that early. We would return to pick her up in time for Sunday school at nine forty-five and morning worship at eleven.

Early April 22, Easter morning, Larry and I drove to Maranatha Baptist Church. The sunrise service was beautiful. We saw the sky painted pink and gold as the sun came up over the horizon. I remembered what Jesus did for me. The pastor gave a wonderful message, and the songs were victorious. It was chilly outside that Sunday as the sun rose, and the service ended.

The Easter season is a time for good cheer. But what is the purpose behind this time of celebration? A bloody death. What? Why celebrate a death. Well, that is not the whole story. Let's move back to the beginning. The only reason we can celebrate Easter is because of the life of Jesus Christ. He was God in flesh. He was the promised Messiah. He was born of a virgin. He lived a perfect life that was in accordance with God's will. He was crucified for my sins. But the story doesn't end with his death. He overcame the grave and death. He arose to life. He now sits on the right hand of God, making intercession for me. His death and resurrection give me a reason for life. So let's celebrate!

Larry's apartment was not too far from the church, so we went there to wait till it was time for us to pick up his mother for Sunday school and worship. We had about two hours before we needed to get to Evelyn's apartment and return to the church.

I took off my strappy white sandals. We had gotten up so early to be on time for the sunrise service. I was tired. I lay down to take a nap. After a while, Larry joined me on his queen-size bed.

We touched hands, which led to a hug and then a kiss. Our desire grew for each other. French kissing was so exciting. One thing led to another. We were holding and touching each other tenderly, but Larry realized we were going too far. We were not doing what was right for our Lord and each other.

He pushed me gently away. We needed to separate and get our passions under control. We needed to cool it!

MY SMART ROMANCE

This was not the time to be intimate with each other. We wanted to wait till we were married to have sex. We wanted to be faithful to God. Temptation to fulfill our desires had brought us to the edge of a precipice. We could have easily fallen over and "known" each other in the biblical sense. But God's Holy Spirit moved and helped us overcome the temptation. We could have victory over our flesh in Jesus's strength, not our own.

Larry asked me to forgive him for going so far. We both had to ask God to forgive us for being so caught up in the moment and each other that we almost gave up my virginity. Love will wait! After such a worshipful morning how could we so quickly fall into temptation—praise God! He had made a way of escape so we could bear the temptation.

I went to the bathroom down the hall from the bedroom. I fixed myself up. I had to straighten my clothes. I brushed my hair and repaired my makeup. I got myself ready to return to the church.

We went over to Evelyn's apartment and picked her up in time for church. The three of us sat together in the sanctuary. We heard a wonderful resurrection message. After the service, we drove to Joan and Art's home. Denise was glad to see her uncle Larry and her grandmother. The six of us sat around the dining room table and had a delightful Easter meal. Joan had prepared a ham, cheesy potatoes, "Deviled Eggs," hot rolls and butter, and a Jell-O salad. After lunch, we sat and chatted as we ate coconut cake and drank coffee. It was Larry and my first Easter together.

Remember, Satan is always trying to get you to fulfill legitimate desires in the wrong way or at the wrong time. Watch out for that roaring lion. He wants to devour you.

Recipe for Deviled Eggs

Ingredient:

- 1 dozen eggs, hard boiled
- 1/2 cup Miracle Whip
- 2 tablespoons yellow mustard
- 1 teaspoon season salt
- 1/2 teaspoon ground black pepper
- dash hot sauce
- dusting of paprika

Directions:

1. Cut egg in half, long ways.
2. Put yolks in a bowl, and mash with a fork.
3. Add other ingredients, except the paprika, and mix well.
4. Fill egg whites with the yolk mixture.
5. Dust with paprika for color.

CHAPTER 10

Counseling

> Memories are the past
> Dreams are the future.
> Snow is for the winter.
> Rain is for the spring.
> Laughter fills the happy.
> Tears fill the sad.
> Years will see them all in our life.

Pastor Gelina believed that a marriage had a better chance of success if the couple had a time to prepare. So he had counseling sessions with the couples that he would officiate at their wedding. He scheduled four sessions with Larry and me. We would meet him on Saturdays at his church office. He gave us homework to do between our meetings.

> Dear Heavenly Father,
>
> Thank You for sending Pastor Gelina to give us marriage counseling. May we listen and learn from his biblical advice.
> In Jesus's name
> Amen.

At one session, Pastor Gelina talked to us about finances and budgeting. I had never used a budget before. One of our homework assignments was to fill out a budget worksheet. At that time, the monthly rent on Larry's apartment was $425, with water and electricity included. The total living expenses for a month on my homework came out to be $1,023.82. Wow! How times have changed.

Larry and I talked about our finances and tithing after that session. I was saved when I was five years old. I had always had a firm belief that God would take care of all I needed. I started tithing as a child. I would get fifty cents from my parents for allowance, and I gave five cents to Jesus. So it was a permanent habit in my life. Larry was also practicing tithing. Larry and I agreed we would give at least 10 percent of our income to the Lord first before we paid our other obligations. We wanted to give to God as a natural outgrowth of our Christian life. We knew God had given us much, much more then we could ever give. We wanted to give to God's work happily and not grudgingly. We trusted God to take care of us.

We discussed using a credit card. We decided to only use it when absolutely necessary and pay the balance off each month. We wanted to live debt-free. Larry had a small amount of debt when we were engaged. He had bought things on credit for his mother. So we planned to pay off those debts as quickly as we could. We both wanted to owe no man anything but to share the gospel with them.

Pastor Gelina talked to us about settling disagreements. Conflict in marriage is a fact of life. All couples have disagreements. Larry and I are both human beings, imperfect, sinful people whom God graciously loves in spite of our imperfections. We each liked things done our way. Sometimes the way we think things should be done does not agree with how the other person thinks things should be done. The disagreements themselves are not the problem, but our reaction to them can create a big problem. The Bible says, "Do not let the sun go down on your wrath." Both Larry and I are very opinionated, which can lead to some loud discussions of our differences. Sometimes we have to agree to disagree.

We must try not to attack the other person during a disagreement but focus on the problem. Walking away and cooling down

MY SMART ROMANCE

sometimes is a good idea when a conflict seems to be escalating. When we are less agitated, we needed to listen to each other's opinion.

Pastor talked to us about making the Lord the center of our home. Both Larry and I loved the Word of God and were committed to studying the Bible. Larry was still taking Bible courses at Washington Bible College. We also knew that attendance at church was a priority for both of us. We wanted to keep growing in the grace and knowledge of the Lord Jesus Christ. We planned to attend Larry's church after we got married.

In my journal I wrote:

> Because I have placed my faith and trust in Christ, Who died and rose and is now at the right hand of God, I know… Nothing can separate me from the love of Christ
>
> — Not death
> — Not life
> — Not angels, principalities, or powers
> — Not things present
> — Not things to come
> — Not height or depth
> — Not any other creature
>
> Because none of these things can separate me from God's love, I can be MORE than a conqueror in all these things.

I wrote down fifteen words that I thought described Larry: strong, godly, faithful, friend, great singer, handy, talented, protective, finisher, responsible, generous, handsome, perfectionist, fastidious, provider. Some of these good qualities, when taken to an extreme, can be hard to deal with. God has to teach me to not take offense and not get upset with a fastidious perfectionist.

Pastor Gelina gave us a personality test on a Wednesday night, then he discussed the results with us the next Saturday. I failed! The test said I would be hard to live with because I was very stubborn and opinionated. Well, I do think there is right and wrong. Usually, my way is the right way, and everyone else's way is the wrong way. Poor Larry was told this before we were married. But he still was willing to marry me.

> Dear Father, I am a very strong-willed child. I know it is hard to deal with a child who wants to do everything her way. Please help me to replace my will with Your perfect will.
> Amen.

In the back of a workbook titled *Before You Say "I Do,"* Larry wrote:

> Why am I marrying Terri? Because I can see the Love for our Lord Jesus Christ in her life by her actions and by her works. She really shows to me that she will be a wonderful Christian woman to share the rest of my life with. She has a love for God's Word. She wants to read His Word faithfully and prays. This is a sign of her maturity in the Christian life. She has a caring spirit and a good teaching gift I believe will make her a good mother for our children.
> Why does Terri want to marry me? Because I have a Love for Jesus, and I want to put Him first in my life. I have a love for God's Word. I believe because I'm faithful to the church that I will be a faithful husband to my family. I love children very much. I want to bring them up in the nurture and admonition of the Lord.

At the last counseling session, Pastor Gelina talked to us about becoming one flesh. He gave us a book as a wedding gift from his wife and him. It was titled *Intended for Pleasure* by Ed Wheat, MD,

MY SMART ROMANCE

and Gaye Wheat. Pastor Gelina wrote this message in the front of our book: "With our best interest in your blessed and radiantly delightful wedded life together in Christ. Pastor and Mrs. Gelina."

The preface of the book by the Wheats ends with this bit of wisdom: "As we begin, please keep one tremendous fact in view: God Himself intended sex for our delight. It was His gift to us—intended for pleasure." This helpful book was written to guide married couples to see sex as a gift from God. Dr. Wheat explained things from a medical and Christian point of view.

We prayed the counseling would do its job and prepare us for our married life. There would still be surprises along the way. We were two different people from two different backgrounds. We definitely did not think the same way. God has to give grace so we can treat each other in a kind manner when what we do rubs the other the wrong way.

Marriage can be like dump cake. You put everything in and mix it up, and out comes something sweet. Marriage may be made in heaven, but we are responsible for the maintenance work.

Recipe for Dump in the Pan Chocolate Cake

Ingredients:

- 3 cups flour
- 2 cups sugar
- 1 teaspoon salt
- 2 teaspoons baking soda
- 1/3 cup cocoa
- 1 teaspoon vanilla
- 1 teaspoon vinegar
- 1/4 cup oil
- 2 cups cold water

Directions:

1. Preheat oven to 350 degrees Fahrenheit.
2. Sift together into the pan the first five ingredients.
3. Make three little mounds of the dry ingredients, and make a hole in each mound.
4. In the first hole, put the vanilla. In the second hole, put the vinegar. In the third hole, put the oil.
5. Over top of everything, pour the water.
6. Stir till well mixed.
7. Bake for about 30 minutes.

One summer, while visiting my grandmother Cassie in Minnesota I tried to make this cake. I misread the directions that had a small *t* in front of the salt and soda. I used a tablespoon of each of those ingredients. We had to end up making three cakes so they would taste right. A tablespoon has three teaspoons in it. That was the day I learned a capital *T* stood for tablespoon, and a lowercase *t* stood for teaspoon in a recipe.

CHAPTER 11

Fixing Up Our New Home

It was an adventure to try to get our first home put together. Well, Larry had been a bachelor for many years. He was already living in the apartment we would be sharing after our honeymoon. I had a lot of things to move into his one-bedroom apartment to make it my home also. How could we fit it all together? How could this space become our nest?

Home
Safe, Secure
Refuge, Relax, Refresh
Meals, Meetings, Merriment, Memories
Clean, Cool, Calm
Family, Friends
Home

We looked around Larry's bedroom and decided we needed more closet space. I had a lot of clothes to move in. There was no place to put them. So we planned to make a closet against the long bare wall in the bedroom. Larry and I went to Lowe's and purchased a closet you could assemble. We worked together to put it up against the wall of his bedroom. Larry did not like to read the instructions. I always want to follow the directions and rules. So two hard heads started arguing about how to make the closet. Finally, we kissed and made up, and the closet got put together.

While working on the closet, Larry told me about living with his dad. When he was thirteen, he was living with his father. His parents had divorced. Larry felt his mother had abandoned him. Larry's mother had taken her little daughter, Brenda, but not him when his parents separated. He did not understand why she did that.

Larry and his father, Thomas Packard, lived in a rooming house in Washington, DC. On the second floor of that house, they had a big one-room apartment. There was a bed in the corner that Larry and his dad shared. They had a two-burner hot plate to cook their food on. There was a little refrigerator. They had a small table with two wooden chairs near the wall. They shared the bathroom with all the other residents of the second floor. The rent was to be paid weekly to the "Old Lady" who owned the house. Some weeks she had trouble getting the rent from Larry's dad.

Larry worked hard to keep their room clean. He washed dishes, made the bed, and swept the floors. He would have to take the trash out in the alley behind the rooming house each day. There were big rats all over in that alley. So Larry stood back and threw the trash as far as he could into the trash can so he would not have to get near the rats.

Larry would iron his father's clothes for him. When we met, the only thing Larry had of his dad's was the old iron. Maybe that was why he always sent his shirts to be pressed and starched at the dry cleaners.

Larry's dad always bought him model cars to build. He had a whole collection of them. On Saturdays, his dad took him to the arcade. Larry was left to play pinball, while his dad went into the adult movie theater to watch a movie. Larry became a pinball wizard.

When the hardware and closet clothing bar were up, I sewed a curtain to cover up the clothes hung in the closet space. I used a queen-size blue bedsheet to make the curtain. We hung it by gold rings on a curtain rod. The gold rings would make a tinkling noise when you moved the curtain back and forth on its rod. Finally, I was able to start moving my clothes to Larry's apartment.

MY SMART ROMANCE

Larry had very little in the way of kitchenware. He had one frying pan to fry potatoes. He had one saucepan to boil his instant rice. His mother had given these to him from her extra pans. I had a very nice set of matching pans from the time I lived alone in my apartment in Pittsburgh. I brought my electric skillet that I loved to use for making "Beef Stroganoff" out of storage. One Saturday, I moved all my pots and pans into the cabinets in Larry's small kitchen.

When I graduated from college, my parents had given me a lovely set of fine china made in Japan. The china plates were octagonal with a lovely Oriental flower pattern called "Geisha." I had dinner plates, salad plates, bowls, teacups and saucers. I unpacked them into the upper shelf in Larry's kitchen. Now we had a service for eight, enough to entertain at our new home.

I hosted a Tupperware party at my parents' home. I had lots of guests from my church and the school. It was a great party. We played games, won prizes, and had good food. The guest ordered lots of Tupperware. I had enough sales at my party that I earned a lot of hostess points from Tupperware. I redeemed the points on a set of flatware for twelve. It was a very nice silver flatware set, with a beautiful floral pattern on the handles. I put those silver utensils in the drawer in the kitchen of Larry's apartment.

Larry helped me move into the living room my Waterfall Front desk and its chair. When I was in college, I often stayed with my Aunt Bessie and Uncle Earl. They lived about an hour away from my college in Mechanicsburg, Ohio. My grandmother's house was on the same lot just a short sidewalk away from her daughter Bessie's home. I had told my uncle I needed a desk. He went every week to auctions and sales. Uncle Earl located the waterfall front desk and chair for me at one of those auctions. It made my desk very special to me.

As we looked around the apartment, we realized we needed some shelves in the living room. I had a lot of books to bring over from my parents' home. So we made bookshelves from white cement construction blocks and two boards. This shelving worked really well for storing all my books.

TERRI LYNN SMART PACKARD

During the time we were arranging the apartment, Larry told me about his youth. Larry had attended Hart Junior High School in Southeast Washington, DC. Larry was the only white boy in the class. He graduated from ninth grade and was scheduled to attend Ballou High School. Larry never got in trouble at school because he kept to himself. But he was sick of it. So he dropped out of school.

Larry worked hard; he was a hustler even in his youth. When he was young, he sold peanuts at the Griffith Stadium in Washington, DC, with a blind man named Felix. He would stand outside the ball stadium and yell, "Here they are, folks. Get your peanuts here!—freshly roasted, golden, toasted peanuts. Only a dime. Peanuts here. Everyone is looking, but no one is buying. Get your peanuts here!" After selling peanuts, he would get to go into the ballpark and watch the Senators play baseball. Larry always loved baseball. He played little league baseball when he was eight and nine years old in the Walter Johnson League. He was a good outfielder.

Larry also helped sell newspapers on Sundays outside St. Matthew's Cathedral with Mr. Kersey, a cab driver. As the people left the early Mass at the DC cathedral, they would purchase their Sunday paper. At Christmastime, he sold mistletoe at that same location.

Larry started working at Whelan's Drugstore when he was a teenager in 1961. He started out at the lunch counter. In those days, every drugstore had a lunch counter. This was a long counter with stools for the customers to sit on. They served coffee for ten cents a cup. They did a big business at breakfast and lunch at Whelan's. At lunchtime, two colored ladies worked at the sandwich bar, making egg salad, tuna salad, chicken salad and bacon, lettuces, and tomato sandwiches. Larry had shifts where he worked different jobs at the lunch counter. He served the food and at times had to bus the counter.

He put the dishes in a dumb waiter, and they went down to the basement where the dishwashing machine was located. Larry also had to wash dishes, and at times he had to make coffee in the huge coffee maker. That is where Larry started drinking strong black coffee.

Later, Larry moved up to manning the cigar and cigarette counter at Whelan's. He sold tobacco, cigarette paper, and cigars.

MY SMART ROMANCE

He also sold candies and newspapers. The cigarettes were only twenty-five cents a pack. He sold lots of cigarettes. He was working at that counter when he heard on the radio that President Kennedy had been shot in Dallas. Larry was so saddened by the news about the assassination in Texas. When Kennedy's funeral procession went through Washington, Larry was at that drug store window, watching. He saw the caisson with Kennedy's flag-draped coffin pulled by white horses travel down Rhode Island Avenue to St. Matthew's Cathedral. Larry saluted to show his respect for the president.

Larry always loved fancy cars. His parents never owned a car, but Larry got his driver's license as soon as he could. A colored janitor at Whelan's Drugstore had a really nice red Pontiac convertible. That nice man would let Larry drive his car whenever Larry wanted. Larry would cruise around the Washington Mall in that convertible. He was happy to just be driving.

While working at the drugstore, Larry got a call from the hospital. They said his dad was at Casualty Hospital. Larry got permission to leave his job. He hopped on a bus and hurried to the hospital. When he arrived at the hospital, a woman came out of a room and said, "You know, your daddy is dead." This statement hit Larry like a two-by-four over the head. Thomas had died of a heart attack when he was sixty-one years old.

After his father died in 1964, Larry had no place to live. His mother's older sister, Ruby, allowed him to live in her huge house in Northwest Washington, DC. He had to pay her rent to stay there. His aunt was a penny pincher and only allowed this growing sixteen-year-old to have one egg and one piece of toast in the morning for breakfast. So when he turned seventeen, he went to the army induction center in Baltimore, Maryland. He signed up for the United States Army. Because of his young age, his mother had to sign and give permission for Larry to join the army. He left for basic training in October. He rode a bus to Fort Jackson in South Carolina. There they gave Larry a physical and a bunch of shots. Then they cut off all his hair and gave him his uniform. But they did feed him much better on the fort.

Larry had eight weeks of basic training, then he did eight weeks of a wheel vehicle mechanic course. He then was ordered to Fort Knox, Kentucky. He took armor and track vehicle training at Fort Knox. Along with all those classes, Larry earned his GED while he was in the army.

The Vietnam War was in full swing. Larry was put on a navy ship in Oakland, California with all the other army men in his company. They stopped in Honolulu, Pearl Harbor, Okinawa, and Yokohama Japan. They spent a month on that ship before they arrived in Korea. The men got off the ship in Inchon, South Korea. When Larry got to the army base, he was called into his superior officer's office. The officer said, "You are only seventeen. You shouldn't be here."

Larry said, "I am already here. Why send me back?" So Larry stayed and repaired tanks on the thirty-eighth parallel, right on the DMZ in Korea for a year.

My summer jobs, as I was growing up, were varied. I babysat for families from my church. I worked at a day care facility in the summer, watching lots of little children. The children were dropped off at six in the morning and picked up at six at night. I was the one raising those little ones. That summer job reinforced my resolve to not put my children into childcare but to be at home with my babies. I wanted to be there for my children. Another summer, I was a nanny for three children while their parent worked. My duties included watching the children, cleaning the house, and cooking. I was also a waitress at an ice-cream parlor for one summer. That was a sticky job. I once tipped a whole tray of ice cream sundaes onto myself as I put them at the customer's table.

I worked while I was in college. I did housekeeping for one year. I cleaned the bathrooms, laundry room, and ran the vacuum up and down the halls of a dorm. I also was a resident adviser another year at Cedarville College. I helped the girls and kept an eye on them in the dorm. I learned a lot from all those work experiences.

Finally, after weeks of hard work, we had all the preparation done on the apartment in Alexandria, so I could move right in and live there after our wedding. Everything looked really nice. This would be our first home as a Packard family.

MY SMART ROMANCE

Dear Lord,

Please bless this home. We want you to be glorified, dear Lord, in our home.

Your children,
Larry and Terri,

Amen.

Recipe for Beef Stroganoff

Ingredients:

- 1 pound beefsteak, thinly sliced
- 1 onion, chopped
- 1 clove garlic, crushed
- 1 tablespoon butter
- 2 cups water
- 1 cube beef bullion
- salt and pepper to taste
- 1 cup sliced fresh mushrooms
- 1 teaspoon cornstarch
- 1/4 cup water
- 1 1/2 cup sour cream

Directions:

1. In an electric skillet, melt butter. Brown beef, onion, and garlic.
2. Deglaze pan with 2 cups of water and bullion.
3. Cover and simmer for about 20 minutes or until beef is tender. Add water if pan becomes too dry so there are always about 2 cups of liquid.
4. Add mushrooms. Cover and steam for 5 minutes.
5. Stir cornstarch and 1/4 cup cold water together, and add to liquid in the pan to thicken. Stir for about 1 minute.
6. Stir in sour cream. Heat till just warm.
7. Serve over wide noodles.

CHAPTER 12

Showers and Rehearsal

Larry's brother-in-law, Art Yow, volunteered to do my bridal portraits. I brought my wedding dress, veil, and flowers to his home on May 12. His wife, Joan, helped him stage the photo shoots. They had the most beautiful azaleas in bloom in their backyard, so Art used the azaleas as a background for most of my pictures. My colorful bouquet looked like it just belonged in their garden. The colorful flowers set off my white wedding dress and veil beautifully.

I wrote this in my journal the night of May 13:

> Look into this microscope
> that looks at the tiny,
> Plants and animals abound.
> My God created these for His pleasure.
> Look into this telescope
> that looks at the immense,
> Planets and stars here abound.
> My God created these for His pleasure.

The ladies of my church planned a bridal shower for me. It was held in the church fellowship hall the evening of May 25. I dressed up in a nice dress. I was wearing pantyhose and high-heeled dress sandals. This was not a casual party but a true dress-up occasion. I was the guest of honor.

At the shower, Cindy Voltz, a family friend, was in charge of the entertainment. She led the ladies in making me a scrapbook. The women were paired up and told a time in my life to represent with their pages of my scrapbook. Then they were given blank scrapbook pages, a stack of magazines, a pair of scissors, and a bottle of glue. Each group of ladies decided what they wanted to put on their blank pages. The room was filled with giggles and laughter as the ladies went to work. The scissors snipped, and the magazines pictures were cut apart and affixed to the pages.

After the pages were finished, they were all assembled into a book. The title of the book was "Terri Smart Packard, This is Your Life!" Cindy read the book to all the ladies and showed us the pictures. The ladies had made twenty-one pages, front and back. My life story was a thick book.

The first page was to represent my babyhood. It had a picture of a baby playing with a ball she was putting in a bowl. The caption the ladies added said, "You will see that the sphere that I hold in my hand will displace its own volume in the yellow bowl." They were poking fun at my being a scientist and my intelligence since I was little. Probably it was also a jab at my last name, Smart.

A page had a magazine picture of a little girl clasping her hands tightly in front of her. The ladies added this caption: "Playing Button, Button who has the button." This had been a favorite game of mine when I was a very little girl.

One page talked about me being "Ready for Camp High Point!" When I was in sixth grade, I went to Camp High Point one summer in Pennsylvania. It was a good Bible camp, but I was really homesick that week of camp. I always had a hard time staying away from home and my mother. At camp, I won a camp T-shirt in the sword drill competition. My Bible was my Sword. The announcer would give a scripture reference and then say, "Swords Up!" The campers would hold up their Bibles and repeat the reference. Then the announcer would say, "Charge!" Each camper searched for that Bible verse. I was the fastest at finding references in my Bible.

Another page about junior-high days had magazine pictures of insects, and the caption said, "Even in Jr. High—Bugs were her bag!"

Science was always my favorite subject. My worst subject was spelling. I was not very good at spelling. I still have trouble with it.

A page representing my high school days had the caption, "Whatever you, do don't forget PERU!" This referred to our family trip to Peru to visit missionary friends the Christmas of my junior year in high school. My family flew to Lima, Peru, and a sweet missionary family we had never met picked us up at the airport. That family let us stay with them for the day because there was no flight out of the Lima airport till the next day. Lima was a hot, dry, and dusty place. I saw poinsettias as large as trees lining the streets of Lima. They were beautiful with their bright red flowers, blooming just in time for Christmas.

From Lima, we flew on to Iquitos, Peru. Carol Ciocca met us at that airport. Carol had been a teacher at Evangel Christian School in Dale City. She had lived with my family in Virginia while she worked at the school. She felt like part of my family, even if we were not related by blood. We were sisters in the Lord.

We stayed in Iquitos at the mission house, where Carol lived, for a week. My sister and I slept in a guest room that had lizards crawling up the walls at night. During our stay in Iquitos, we did many new things. We visited the church where Carol ministered. My father preached in English, and a translator shared what he said to the congregation in Spanish. Rhonda and I sang for the church.

We went to the local outdoor market with Carol shopping. It was not like going to the grocery shop at home. There were chickens in crates to be bought alive. Fresh red meat was hanging from hooks over the stands. At this market, I saw piles of trash just thrown on the street, with vultures sitting on top of the garbage. Peru felt very exotic to this teenager.

My parents were always showing their gift of hospitality. All my growing up years, they had missionaries staying at our home whenever they were in our area. One of the missionary families that always stayed with us were Dan and Judy Smith. They were missionaries on the Amazon River in Peru. They lived on a houseboat with their three young children. They invited my family to travel with them down the Amazon River for a few days. To get on the houseboat, you had to climb from the muddy shore up a narrow wooden plank. It was a bit scary, but I did not look down, and I made it onto the boat.

Traveling along the Amazon, we saw the rainforest crowding in along the riverbanks. I saw beautiful bright-colored orchids hanging from the trees. There were river porpoises playing in the water. We ate fish caught fresh from the river. We met a man who had his hand all bandages from being attacked by a piranha caught in his fishing net.

When we stopped at a village, I played games with the native children. I had so much fun running and playing tag. When I sat down to rest because I was so hot, the children offered me a cup of water. It was straight from the river. I had to graciously refuse. I did not tell them I could not drink their water, or I would get sick.

We went to worship services in thatched huts. We sang the same songs in Spanish that we sang at our church in English. How wonderful to know my Christian family spanned across the globe.

On our cruise back to Iquitos, we donned life jackets and jumped off the front of the boat into the Nini River that runs into the Amazon. We floated with the current and caught a rope floating behind the houseboat. Then we pulled ourselves hand over hand back to the boat. We climbed out of the Nini River and ran to the front of the boat and did it all over again. I was swimming in a jungle river in "deepest, darkest Peru," as Paddington would say.

Christmas in Peru is a little different than in the United States. There is no snow; it is too hot. There were no pine trees to make into Christmas trees. We did have panettone, an Italian Christmas bread, for the first time while in Peru. There was an Italian bakery just down the road from the mission home. The panettone was always so fresh and delicious.

We brought gifts from the states to share with the missionaries. We bought things they could not get in Peru. On Christmas Day, all the missionaries in the area met at a restaurant. We had a grand feast of Peruvian roasted chicken and fried plantain. We sang Christmas carols together in English.

When it was time to return to the United States, our friend, Carol Ciocca, came back with us. She was having some medical

MY SMART ROMANCE

issues, and we were able to help her travel home safely. We flew back to Florida. We were met by my Uncle Earl and Aunt Bessie in their camper. We visited an orange grove and went to Disneyland while we were in Florida. What an adventure our family's mission trip to Peru was.

The ladies at my bridal shower made pages about my college years at Cedarville College in Ohio. There was a page about my graduate school time in the lab at University of Pittsburgh. They were trying to include everything about my life in that scrapbook.

Later, a page with a boat had this caption cut out of different sayings from the magazines: "A cruise on the 'Love Boat' got her in the mood for a taste of things to come." They were referring to my trip on the Norwegian Cruise Line ship, the Song of America. I had taken the cruise with my parents from Florida to the Caribbean the year before I started teaching at Evangel Christian School. It was supposed to be an anniversary trip for my parents, but they allowed me to tag along. I had an upper bunk in their stateroom. We had a super week together. I loved swimming in the saltwater pool on the ship. We enjoyed watching a crew member carve giant ice sculptures to be used on the midnight buffets. How could he make a dolphin from that huge block of ice?

The evening meal on the cruise ship was formal. We dressed up in our best every evening. Each person was assigned a table and a time to have their dinner. My parents and I were seated at a table with five other passengers. Every night, a young lady named Cheryl sat next to me at the table. She was on the cruise with her grandmother and an older aunt. Her grandmother and aunt enjoyed taking thing easy. They liked sitting on the deck during the day. Cheryl did not find that very exciting. Since she was close to my age, we hung out together that whole week of the cruise.

My parents, Cheryl. and I were able to visit St. Thomas. We sunned on the pristine beaches and swam in the crystal-clear water. We took a boat excursion to a private island. At San Juan, we disembarked and visited the old fort. We climbed up the hill through the winding narrow streets. You could see for a long way out into the ocean from the fort.

One night on the ship, there was a costume ball, where we dressed up in costumes we made. My parents won a prize because they had such a cute outfit. They dressed up as zookeepers. My father had on red shorts, a big straw hat, and a fake black mustache pasted on his lip. My mother had on a peasant outfit. Her long skirt had multiple layers with bright-colored material. Both Mom and Dad had stuffed-toy monkeys with long legs and arms draped around their shoulders.

One page of my bridal shower book said, "She met Larry and realized... There Is Only One." It was true; Larry was the only one for me. God had planned this man just for me. God knew we needed each other to be able to serve Him in the way that was best for both of us.

The next picture in the book they made was of a man resting in a recliner. The man was to represent my father. The caption by the picture read, "As Ira was relaxing, she broke the news to him. Finally, he agreed and said, 'Two dips are better than one.'" This page really made all the ladies at my bridal shower laugh.

The scrapbook went on to plan Larry and my future life together. "She finally caught Him!" and "He Got Smart!" were fun pages of the book. The ladies included these passages: "The wife shall be as a fruitful vine... Blessed is he that has his quiver full!" with pictures of lots of children. Maybe the ladies were being prophets.

The last page in my life-story scrapbook had an older couple with their foreheads touching and looking into each other's eyes. The article from the magazine started, "He still sees the woman he fell in love with." The caption my friends added was, "Love still in bloom."

After the fun of creating the scrapbook, Ruth Gelina, my pastor's wife, gave a devotional. She had always been an example to me of a godly woman, like the Proverbs 31 woman. When I was young, I sat behind her at church, and I would watch her. She was a schoolteacher, a pastor's wife, a mother, a Sunday school teacher, and a very sweet lady. I was glad she shared from God's Word at my bridal shower.

The ladies had ordered a lovely sheet cake for the party. It had a pink border and pink roses on the top of the cake. Besides the cake, we had punch and snacks to eat. The ladies at my party were so generous. I had lots of gifts to open that night. Then I had lots of thank-you notes to write afterward.

Dear Heavenly Father,

Thank You! I will consciously give You thanks for all that is brought into my life. Each occasion of pain makes me more sensitive to others hurts. Each occasion of joy helps me lift the spirits of others. All things, and I mean all things, work together for the maturing and perfecting of the saints.

Love,
Terri

Larry also had a bachelor party before our wedding. His best man and brother-in-law, Art, hosted the bachelor dinner. Art sent our invitations to Larry's friends (probably Joan wrote them). The dinner was at 6:30 p.m., Saturday, June 16. The dinner was at Art's home in Potomac, Maryland. Joan cooked the dinner for the men. Larry had a nice time with his guy friends.

The RSVPs and regrets started to arrive from our wedding invitations. My father's sister, Aunt Bessie, and her husband, Uncle Earl Fox, were coming from Ohio with my grandmother, Lily Smart.

They were bringing my cousin Sharon and her children Robin, Chad, and Stephanie to the wedding. My bridesmaid, Faye, and her husband were coming. My third freshman college roommate, Kathy Lloyd, was coming with her husband to the ceremony.

My mother's sister, Aunt Marilyn, and her husband, Uncle Jr, were planning to come from Minnesota to the wedding. But my parents received a distressing call from Marilyn and Jr. Their daughter, Roxanne, who was about my age, had tried to commit suicide. She took her shotgun and put it under her chin to shoot her head off. But as she pulled the trigger, she must have had regrets because she moved the gun and only shot her jaw off. She was in the hospital in Minnesota, having multiple surgeries to repair her face. This terrible news was a shock to us all. It put a cloud over our happy wedding preparations.

I remembered being little in Minnesota, maybe two or three years old. The dirt street was filled with puddles. The rain had filled every low spot in the road. It was such a beautiful sight, the sun sparkling on the hundreds of tiny lakes. I could not wait to get out and play. My cousin Roxanne and I collected as many popsicle sticks as we could find off the ground surrounding the front of my parents' grocery, The Smart Store. Then we sat down near that biggest puddle and started floating our boats. We did not care how wet or how muddy we got. We were having so much fun.

Out of the store came my mother. "What are you two doing in the middle of the street?" she exclaimed. "Do you want to get run over?" She dragged us out of the street. What a loss. All those popsicle boats and water to play in, and I was not allowed to play in the middle of the street. I also had a habit of going outside and turning the hose on any customers trying to enter my parents' store. I thought watering the people was super fun.

Later, when Roxy and I were a little older, I arrived at my grandma Cassie's from Illinois. Roxy informed me we were going to play a while and fight a while. We were in a little bedroom, playing on the floor with toys when, all of a sudden, Roxy knocked me over and sat on me. She said, "We played, and now we are going to fight."

My sister, Rhonda, drove all the way from Minnesota with her boyfriend, Wes, for my wedding. They made it in time to help with some of the wedding preparations. I wrote a poem for my sister, the nurse.

Healing, Helping, Caring

Your hands are cool on the fevered brow,
Your voice is calm and reassuring.
Your eyes are quick to smile and cheer.

You make the lonely feel loved.
You make the hopeless look up for strength.
You make the sad remember the good things in life.

You don't just distribute medicine and leave.
You bring the patient before the Great Physician
        in prayer,
And follow His instructions well.

Where would we put all these people coming for my wedding? Our split-level house had five bedrooms and two bathrooms. Our house could hold a lot of the guests. My parents had a camper that slept at least six. My Uncle Earl and Aunt Bessie brought their camper for the contingency from Ohio. We had a house full of friends and family. Everyone squeezed in somewhere that weekend of my wedding. No one complained about the arrangements; they were so glad to be together.

Thursday, June 21, a crew of us descended on the church to set it up for the wedding. In the sanctuary, we placed live plants and candles around each of the tall windows. We put the artificial flowers up front of the sanctuary. We moved the pulpit off the stage. We put the big antique Bible Larry and I had been given up in the front of the church in a book stand on the communion table. The Bible was open to the "Love Chapter," 1 Corinthians 13.

We arranged the two prayer benches we had rented facing each other on the platform. We set out the candelabra and tied a big, white bow on it. The candles to be lit during the wedding ceremony were put in place. White bows were hung on the end of the pews. Everything looked so beautiful in the sanctuary. The church was ready for the wedding, but was I?

In Martin Hall, the church gym, folding tables and chairs were set up. An archway was constructed in the middle of the floor. Decorations were put up all around. Many people from the church and school helped us prepare the large area. It looked very festive in the fellowship hall.

Then Friday night, we had the wedding rehearsal. When work was over, Larry went home, showered, and dressed at his apartment in Alexandria. Then he rushed down to the church in Dale City. Joan and Art picked up Evelyn and brought her to the rehearsal. My parents brought my sister and me. Faye and her husband drove to the church. Shawne arrived with her father, the pastor. Larry's two attendants each arrived from their jobs. We all made it to the church on time.

Pastor Gelina gave us advice about where to stand. We did not want the regular wedding setup with bridesmaids on the bride's side and the groomsmen on the groom's side. We decided to stand the groomsmen with the bridesmaids one set on each side of the platform. The maid of honor did stand beside the bride. The best man stood beside the groom. The pastor went over the order of the service so we would know when to arrive at the stage and where to go.

We walked through the program to be prepared for Saturday. My father had some trouble remembering what he was to say, but he finally figured it out. Larry practiced singing his solo, "I Could Never Promise You" by Don Francisco, with the pianist. Things went pretty smoothly at the rehearsal. I hoped that meant the wedding service would go smoothly too.

The rehearsal dinner is the responsibility of the groom and his family. So Larry's sister, Joan, and his mother brought dinner to the church. After the rehearsal, everyone ate dinner downstairs in the church. We were in the kindergarten classroom of the school. The tables and chairs were all low to the ground. The seats were great for kindergarten students but a little harder for adults. Evelyn brought her Jell-O salad with little bits. My mother really liked it. Mom had never had anything like it with raisins, walnuts, apples, and mixed fruit studding the red Jell-O like jewels.

Larry and I went to the back parking lot of the church and had a disagreement—the day before our wedding, and we had an argument. (I do not remember what we disagreed about. I asked Larry if he remembered what we argued about. He said, "I don't know what we argued about, but it must have been your fault." That made me laugh.)

MY SMART ROMANCE

Recipe for Evelyn's Jell-O

Ingredients:

- Large box strawberry Jell-O mix
- 1 banana, sliced
- 1 can fruit cocktail, drained
- 1 red apple, cored and diced with skin on
- 1/2 cup raisins
- 1/2 cup chopped walnuts

Directions:

1. Make the Jell-O according to the directions on the box.
2. Stir in all the other ingredients. (Evelyn called these the "little bits.")
3. Refrigerate.

CHAPTER 13

The Wedding

Finally, our big day arrived. June twenty-third, the sun came up on a beautiful day—no clouds, no rain. My little blue Datsun was all packed with our suitcases ready for us to leave on our honeymoon after the celebrations of the day. Larry hid his Camaro. He was afraid it would be decorated and messed up. Maybe his yellow paint would be written on if any of my students knew where his car was. My father lent Larry his old car so we could leave the church after the wedding reception.

Early in the morning, the baker arrived at the church and set up the tall wedding cake on the table under the arch. The food for the reception was put in the church kitchen refrigerator. My dad went to the grocery store to pick up the hundreds of rolls that had been ordered for the sandwiches to be served at our wedding reception. The final preparations were falling into place.

My bridesmaids, my mother, and I assembled in the women's bathroom in the church basement. It was a large bathroom with a long sink and mirror area. We were all so excited. We did our makeup and got dressed, helping each other with buttons and sashes. My mother arranged my flower crown and veil on my brown curls for me.

Larry and my father were in the men's bathroom before the service was to begin. Larry kept tugging at his tuxedo pants. They seemed so short. The whole suit did not seem to fit him well. Ira kept trying to pull his pants up; they were too long. His jacket sleeves

106

MY SMART ROMANCE

came down over his hands. The men decided to try trading outfits. After the switch, their pants and jackets were just right. They felt much better. The tuxedo rental company had mixed up their suit orders. They were so glad they figured out the problem before they needed to walk down the aisle.

People started arriving thirty minutes before the ceremony was to begin. The ushers kept seating people. The church was packed! Over three hundred people came to our wedding. The pianist played beautiful hymns and classical music before the service.

My mother and Larry's mother were escorted up to the front of the church by the ushers at the right time. Our mothers each lit a candle on the outsides of the central candelabra. Then they were seated in the front row of the church.

Larry waited at the door as his best man, Art, fixed his tie and got him ready to enter the sanctuary. Then Larry walked to the front of the church to wait with Pastor Gelina for the rest of the wedding party. As the organ music started, the bridesmaids were escorted by the groomsmen to their places on the platform at the front of the church. My maid of honor marched slowly in with the best man to the front of the church, and they took their places on either side of the pastor.

As my father and I were standing at the door, ready to enter the church and walk down the aisle, I was so nervous. I turned to my father and said, "I have to go to the bathroom."

He commanded me, "No! You don't!" (My sister thinks this is so funny because our father never told us no. He always let us do what we wanted.) A few rocky moments like that can end up making the day full of sweet memories. It is kind of like my favorite cookies, "Raisin Rocks."

The wedding march started on the organ, with the famous chords of "Here Comes the Bride." Then my father took my arm, and we started a slow march to the front of the church. All the people stood up and turned to look at us walking down the aisle.

Adorned in a flowing white wedding gown with a lacy veil on my head, I swept down the aisle of the church, surrounded by flowers. At the altar, there stood this strikingly handsome prince of a man.

Our eyes met, and the lightning of love flashed between us. It was my dream! God had given me the desire of my heart.

As Larry saw me coming down the aisle, he was happy and thankful. He thought God had given him a treasure "far above rubies."

My father and I stopped at the bottom of the steps up to the platform, where Larry was waiting for me. Pastor Gelina addressed the assembled company and said, "Dearly beloved, we are gathered here in the sight of God and in the face of this company to join together Larry Packard and Terri Smart in holy matrimony." Then the pastor asked if anyone knew a reason we should not be married. Since no one stood up and shouted, the ceremony went on.

The pastor asked, "Who gives this woman to be married to this man?"

My father got it right and said, "Her mother and I do." Then my father placed my right hand into Larry's hand. Larry and I walked up the stairs to the platform. I handed my bouquet to my sister. Larry and I stood looking at each other, while my father went and sat down next to my mother.

Pastor Gelina said a prayer in which he thanked God for this marriage. Then Pastor Bill McLean, Larry's dear friend, came up to the platform and gave a devotional. Pastor McLean talked about Jesus Christ as the bridegroom and about Jesus's bride. Jesus's bride was not like Larry's bride. Jesus's bride was not desirable or lovely. They were like sheep gone astray, but Jesus loved them in spite of it. His love was not enough though. Because Jesus was holy, and in His justice, the sin had to be condemned, grace was what abounded. Jesus died for our sins. He paid our penalty and died on the cross, and three days later, He was resurrected. This great love story is for each of us sinners. One day, the trumpet will sound, and the bride will meet the Lord in the air to live with Jesus for eternity. Pastor McLean gave an invitation to accept Christ as Savior and be part of that bride with a home in heaven.

When Pastor McLean sat down, Pastor Gelina asked Larry if he would take me as his wife and promise to fulfill all the duties of a husband and provide for me as best he could. Larry said, "I do."

MY SMART ROMANCE

Pastor Gelina asked me if I would take Larry as my husband and promise to fulfill the duties of a wife, to love him, comfort him, to obey him, to honor, and keep him in sickness and in health. I said, "I do."

Then we exchanged rings. Larry repeated after the pastor as he put the ring on my hand.

"I, Larry Packard, take thee, Terri Smart, to be my wedded wife, to have and to hold from this day forward for better, for worse, for richer, for poorer, in sickness, and in health to love and to cherish till death us do part, and with this ring I thee wed."

Then I was handed Larry's ring to put on his hand as I repeated after the minister the pledge. "I, Terri Smart, take thee, Larry Packard, to be my wedded husband, to have and to hold from this day forward for better, for worse, for richer, for poorer, in sickness, and in health to love and to cherish till death us do part, and with this ring I thee wed."

Larry and I stood holding hands and looking deeply into each other's eyes as Larry sang to me.

> I could never promise you on just my strength
>   alone,
> that all my life I'd care for you and love you as
>   my own.
> I've never known the future I only see today
> the words that last a lifetime
> are words I'm going to do.

Here, Larry laughed because he had mixed up the words and sang the ending to the second verse on the first verse. Our eyes twinkled as we realized his error. But Larry went on to the second verse with only the little laugh and smile between us. I do not think anyone in the congregation even knew of his mistake. Larry sang on.

> But the love inside my heart today is more than
>   mine alone—
> it never changes, never fail, it never seeks its own,

And by the God who gives it and who lives in me
    and you,
I know the words I speak today are words I'm
    going to do.

So I stand before you now for all to hear and see,
and promise you in Jesus name the love He's
    given me,
and through the years on earth, and as eternity
    goes by,
the life and love He's given us are never going to
    die.

After Larry sang, the pastor pronounced us husband and wife at 11:02 a.m. on the twenty-third day of June in the year of our Lord, one thousand nine hundred and eighty-four. Pastor Gelina said, "What therefore God hath joined together, let not man put asunder."

Then the focus of the ceremony turned to the candles in the standing candelabrum. The pastor said, "The outside candles of the candelabra have been lighted by the respective mothers to represent Larry and Terri's lives to this moment. They are two distinct lights, each capable of going their separate ways. To bring bliss and happiness to their home, there must be the merging of these two lights into one light. This is what the Lord meant when He said, 'For this cause shall a man leave father and mother, and shall cleave to his wife: and they twain shall be one flesh.' From now on, their thoughts shall be for each other rather than for their individual selves. Their plans shall be mutual. Their joys and sorrows shall be shared alike.

"As each takes a candle and together light the center one, they will extinguish their own candles, thus letting the center candle represent the union of their lives into one flesh. As this one light cannot be divided, neither shall their lives be divided but be a united testimony in a Christian home. May the radiance of this one light be a testimony of their unity in the Lord Jesus Christ."

As the pastor spoke, Larry and I each took a candle and held it up to the center candle. Then we blew out the candles we were

MY SMART ROMANCE

holding and placed them back in the candelabra. It was a very meaningful moment.

Larry and I then held hands and faced the minister. Pastor Gelina said, "I charge you, as you hope for happiness in your married life, to be true to the vows you have taken. You now begin life under new conditions and with larger responsibilities, and it is only by faithfully performing the duties and fulfilling the obligations of this new relation that true and lasting happiness can be found.

"Larry, guard well this woman, who now commits herself to your keeping and strive so to live that no word or deed of yours shall cloud her brow with sorrow or dim her eyes with tears of grief.

"Terri, strive to retain by your virtues the heart you have won by your graces.

"Let not your voices lose the tender tone of affection. Let not 'your eyes forget the gentle ray they wore in courtship's smiling day.' So may you find in your union an unfailing source of joy.

In setting up of the Christina Home, there is a book, which the Lord has prepared for His children to guide and instruct them in every detail of their homelife. It was Joshua of old who heard the Lord say, 'This book of the law shall not depart out of thy month; but thou shalt meditate therein day and night, that thou mayest observe to do according to all that is written therein: for then thou shalt make thy way prosperous and then thou shalt have good success. Have not I commanded thee? Be strong and of a good courage; be not afraid, neither be thou dismayed: for the LORD thy God is with thee withersoever thou goest.'

"We know you each have your own Bible for your private devotion and study, but this occasion calls for a special Bible, a family Bible, one not just to record your family, births, and deaths, but one used in your family devotions. We suggest that you begin this day reading together, praying together, living together according to God's Word, and that you continue this plan each day you are together, until Jesus comes.

"This Bible is committed to your keeping, Brother Larry, for you are the head of the new home you two are now establishing. May

God, the Author and Finisher of your faith, guide you through its use to that perfect wisdom revealed herein."

Larry and I changed our focus from the Bible to the pastor.

"Let us all unite our hearts in prayer of dedication of our brother and sister."

Larry and I moved and knelt on the kneeling benches facing each other. Pastor McLean returned to the stage and prayed for us and our marriage. After the prayer, Larry helped me stand up from the bench, and my sister handed me my bouquet.

Larry and I stood and faced the guest, filling the auditorium, and Pastor Gelina said, "I present to you, Mr. and Mrs. Larry Packard."

We walked down the right aisle of the church, holding hands and smiling from ear to ear. Our attendants followed us out of the church two by two into the foyer.

Wait a minute, what about the kiss? I don't think I got one! We never heard those sweet words, "You many kiss the bride." So maybe there was no kiss. I think I was cheated!

MY SMART ROMANCE

Recipe for Raisin Rocks

Ingredients:

- 1 1/2 cups sugar
- 1 cup shortening
- 2 or 3 eggs
- 1 cup raisins
- 3/4 cup raisin juice
- 1 teaspoon baking soda
- 3 cups flour or more flour as needed
- 1 teaspoon baking powder
- 1 teaspoon cinnamon
- 1 teaspoon cloves

Directions:

1. Preheat oven to 350 degrees Fahrenheit. Grease cookie sheets.
2. Place raisins in a saucepan and cover with water. Boil. Drain raisins, reserving the needed 3/4 cup of juice.
3. Add the baking soda to the raisin juice. It will bubble up. (This is fun to watch.) Put the plump raisins back in the juice.
4. Beat sugar, shortening, and eggs till fluffy.
5. Add raisin mix to sugar mix and stir.
6. Add all remaining ingredients and stir.
7. Drop onto prepared cookie sheets.
8. Bake about 12 minutes till golden brown.

These cookies are supersoft and sweet. They are not hard like rocks at all. My mother says these cookies should have more raisins in the recipe. So if you want, add more raisins.

CHAPTER 14

The Reception

After receiving congratulations and shaking all those hands in the receiving line, we had group pictures taken by the photographer up in the sanctuary. My mother wore blue, and Larry's mother wore pink. My grandmother Smart was also in a pink dress. (She was the only grandparent either Larry or I had alive.) The men in their gray and the women in their pastel colors made a colorful group. The photographer lined everyone up and snapped the picture. Then the photographer rearranged the families and snapped another and another and another. The pictures seemed to take forever. We endured because we wanted the photos to remember this special day.

While the pictures were being taken, the guests were filling their plates and listening to praise music in the fellowship hall. Children were cutting lollipops off the lollipop tree set up just for them. Everyone seemed to be talking at the same time. The wedding guests were having a great time. The fellowship hall was filled to capacity.

Finally, when the photos were over, we went down the stairs to the fellowship hall. The emcee stopped the praise music that was playing in the background and announced the wedding party. All the people in the fellowship hall stood up and cheered for us as we entered. The music started again, and we mingled with all our friends. We moved from table to table, smiling, shaking hands again, and hugging. There were so many people to speak to. We received so many congratulations. People would hand Larry envelopes with money in them. Larry remembers stuffing his jacket pockets with cash.

Sarah Aiken, the six-year-old granddaughter of Eva Aiken, wanted to "see" my wedding dress. Sarah was blind. I let her feel the wide skirt of my dress, and then I bent down so she could feel my hair and my veil. Sarah loved being able to "see" my wedding clothes.

> Out of every kindred, tongue, and nation,
> A people have been redeemed.
> Called and chosen for a special relation.
> Given power to become children of the King.

Dear Heavenly Father,

> Thank You so much for all these people who love You. Thank You that they have a part in our lives.
> In Jesus's name,
> Amen.

Almost all of Larry's family was at the wedding and reception. His best man, Art, and his sister Joan were really involved in our special day. Larry's brother James Packard and his wife, Karen, were there with their sons. Larry' baby sister, Brenda Packard, was there to celebrate with us. But Larry's oldest brother, Danny Packard, did not come to the celebration, even though he was staying at his mother apartment the day of our wedding. I could not understand why Danny would not come. Why did he not want to be at his brother's wedding? I never got to meet Danny, so I guess it will always be something I do not understand.

There was so much food on the serving tables. My mother and Mrs. Aiken had done a wonderful job of catering for the reception. Cut glass punch bowls were filled with salads. Trays were filled with colorful vegetables. Large watermelons cut into bowls were filled to the brim with jewel-toned fruit. There were plenty of freshly baked rolls from the bakery to be made into sandwiches. Some of my students even helped serve the punch and food. Everyone was enjoying lunch seated at the tables, set up in the fellowship hall.

Larry and I do not remember eating anything at our reception. Food was not what was on our mind at that time. But there are pictures of both of us carrying plates of food. So maybe we ate something, but with all the excitement of the day, we did not eat much.

When it was time to cut the cake, Larry and I made it to the middle of the room, where the cake stood on a roundtable under the white trellis we had set up. White paper wedding bells hung from the center of the trellis. The cake was so tall and beautiful, with columns holding up the different layers.

The colorful frosting flowers flowed down the side and stood out against the white frosting. We cut a piece from the bottom layer of the cake, and I carefully tried to feed Larry a bite of cake. But when it was Larry's turn to feed me, he gave me too big a bite of cake and got it on my face. Everyone thought that was great and started laughing.

The bride-and-groom music box cake topper and the top layer of the cake were removed. The top cake was saved for us to have on our first wedding anniversary. The rest of the layers were cut and distributed to the crowd. Larry's sister, Joan, helped cut and serve the cake. She looked lovely in her pink silken dress and big straw hat as she helped with the cake. The guest ate up all that cake.

Before the wedding, Larry and I had decided to save the gifts from the reception and unwrap them when we got back from our honeymoon. We thought unwrapping the gifts would take up too much time. But our plans were changed. My Uncle Earl said he would be insulted if we did not open his gift. So we had to open all the gifts. One of my students from the school sat and made a note of all the gifts and who they were from. Later I wrote thank-you notes to all the people who gave us gifts.

After all the presents, I sat down on a chair under the archway in the middle of the fellowship hall. I gently pulled up the skirt of my dress and revealed my white tights and my ballet slippers. Then Larry knelt down in front of me and removed the blue lace garter I

MY SMART ROMANCE

had on my thigh. He stood up and threw the garter over his shoulder to the crowd of unmarried men. My young cousin Chad, from Ohio, caught it. He held his prize up in the air triumphantly.

I had a little bouquet made that looked like my wedding bouquet. It was to be thrown so I would not give away my silk wedding flowers. All the unmarried girls crowded around as I turned my back to them. I threw the flowers over my shoulder. One of my junior high students caught the flowers. She smiled at her accomplishment, then she had to sit down on the chair I had occupied and have my cousin put the garter on her leg. She and he were so embarrassed that their faces turned dark red.

When we left the church, all the guests filled the main portico to see us on our way. They cheered and threw rice at us. How happy we were to be married.

Dear Heavenly Father,

Thank You for such a beautiful day. God, You have blessed us. We have so many friends and family members praying for our new marriage. May our new family be one that brings glory to Your name.
Amen.

Recipe for Grandma Smart's Homemade Egg Noodles

Ingredients:

- 1 beaten egg
- 2 tablespoons milk
- 1/2 teaspoon salt
- about 1 cup of flour (add more as needed for rolling out)

Instructions:

1. Combine beaten egg, milk. and salt.
2. Add enough flour to make a stiff dough.
3. Roll thin or cheat, like I do, and use the spaghetti maker to roll it out, coating noodles with flour as you put them through the machine.
4. Cut the rolled-out dough into the size noodles you need. (If I want spaghetti, I use the thinner setting on my spaghetti machine. If I want wide noodles, I cut them with a butter knife.)
5. Let the noodles sit awhile and dry. (I usually don't take too long here.)
6. Drop noodles into boiling water or soup.
7. Cook about 10 minutes uncovered.

This makes about 2 cups of noodles. I usually double this recipe when cooking for my whole family.

Grandma Lily and Grandpa Ira Smart always made us big breakfasts whenever we visited them in Ohio. Grandma's breakfast had grapefruits cut in half, fried eggs, and side pork. There were two things I liked about her breakfast (because I did not like fried eggs). The first was to eat the grapefruit out of its skin with her special grapefruit spoons that had a serrated edge to cut into the fruit. The second thing I liked was the side pork; it was like really thick cut bacon. I would eat the pork folded in a piece of bread with mustard on it.

MY SMART ROMANCE

Grandma Smart made the best beef and homemade noodles with this noodle recipe for us when we visited. It was a wonderful dish. I usually make chicken or turkey when I make homemade noodles. I used to start by rolling the noodles out with a rolling pin and cutting them by hand. Now I have gotten lazy and have Larry turn the crank on my spaghetti maker to roll out these noodles.

My Grandpa Ira Smart died when I was six years old. He had just celebrated his ninetieth birthday a short time before he went to heaven.

CHAPTER 15

Honeymoon

When Larry was in the U. S. Army, the last base he was stationed to was Fort Carson in Colorado Springs, Colorado. He loved the area and made trips by himself back to Colorado after leaving the army. He loved to cruise up and down Nevada Avenue in his car, reminiscing about his army days. He wanted me to see the beautiful state. So our plan was to travel to Colorado for our honeymoon in my little blue Datsun.

After the wedding, I changed into my cute blue knit dress. It had a scoop neck and little peplum ruffle and a knit belt to tie at the waist. I had fallen in love with the dress when I found it is a shop. I left my wedding finery for my mother and sister to take care of for me. They were the cleanup crew.

We left Virginia on the way to Colorado with a prayer.

Dear Lord,

Give us traveling mercies. Thank You for our beautiful wedding and that You have given us to each other.
We love You, Lord.
Amen.

MY SMART ROMANCE

The first stop on our road trip was the Penn Alps Inn in Grantsville, Maryland. This was an Amish restaurant that served great home-cooked food. We had our first dinner together as a married couple at that restaurant. We were both starving because we had not had much to eat at our lunch reception. We ate everything on the buffet. There was fried chicken, slices of beef, meat loaf, mashed potatoes, every kind of salad, and all kinds of decadent desserts. After dinner, we walked around the grounds of the inn, holding hands. There were booths set up around the yard with homemade items for sale. The shopkeepers were mostly Amish women with little, white caps on their hair and aprons to cover their dresses. Behind the inn was the historic stone arch of the Casselman River Bridge that led nowhere. The bridge had been built in 1813. Penn Alps Inn was a very historic and scenic place.

Larry did not book a hotel ahead of time because he was unsure how far we would drive that first day of our honeymoon. It started getting dark. We had driven as far as Morgantown, West Virginia.

Larry found the Westover Motel and paid for us a room. We took our luggage into the hotel. I put on my beautiful white negligee. Now we were married, it was the right time to know each other intimately. Proverbs 5:18–19 says, "Rejoice with the wife of your youth. As a loving deer and a graceful doe. Let her breast satisfy you at all times, and always be enraptured with her love."

We had pulled the curtains shut at the hotel window, but the business across the street from the hotel had a flashing neon sign. All night, the room would light up and then go dark as that sign flashed on and off. Neither of us slept well that night. What a way to start a honeymoon.

Each day of our honeymoon, we read the Bible together. We planned to read through Psalms and Proverbs during our first month of marriage. So we started reading Psalm 24 for the day of the month the twenty-fourth. We then added thirty to the date to read that Psalm. Repeating this had us reading five psalms a day. Then at the end of a month, we had read the whole book of Psalms. We also read the Proverbs chapter for the day of the month. The last day, we read the thirtieth and thirty-first chapter of Proverbs, so we could finish it in the month.

> Let's all praise the Lord.
> Praise Him for His strength.
> Praise Him for His grace
> Praise Him for His wonderful love.

> Let's all praise the Lord.
> Praise Him every day,
> For His mercies are new each morning.
> Praise Him along our way.
> Let Him direct our paths.

> Praise Him with your whole heart.
> Praise His name for His loving kindness,
> For He has magnified His Word.
> Let all the kings praise thee, O Lord.

We took the trip to Colorado slowly and stopped along the way to see anything we thought was interesting. The second day, we traveled about five hundred miles. We stayed in Effingham, Illinois. Our third day traveling took us along the Kansas Turnpike traveling from Kansas City to Topeka Kansas for a toll.

We spent that night in Salina, Kansas, at a Travel Lodge. Our hotels were getting a little better, no flashing lights. We had traveled about 550 miles that third day. I was glad our time in the car would soon be over, and we could stretch our legs more.

On Tuesday, the twenty-sixth of June, we arrived in Colorado. We were so excited to be in Colorado. We stopped and took a picture by the rustic wooden sign that said, "Welcome to Colorful Colorado." At Limon, Colorado, we got off Highway 70 and started toward Colorado Springs. Driving along Colorado Highway 24, we made a game of who could see Pikes Peak first. Finally, we spotted the snowy white peak among the clouds in front of us. We knew we were close to our destination now.

MY SMART ROMANCE

We had reservation at the Van Horne Cottages in Manitou Springs, Colorado. Manitou Springs is just to the west of Colorado Springs. We would have a cute little log cabin all to ourselves with a kitchen, living room, bathroom, and bedroom. We arrived at the office of the cottages at about three in the afternoon and went in to pay for our stay. Right outside the office was a little pool with sparkling blue water. I could hardly wait to jump in the water. I love to swim. We drove down a little driveway to our cabin. Larry took the key and opened the door. We were hit with the terrible smell of wet dog. We entered, and the place was filthy. The refrigerator had moldy food in it. The bathroom tub was a brown mess. I tried not to cry. Larry was mad.

Larry went straight up to the office to tell them we could not stay here. We wanted our money back. The manager told Larry we could not have the money back because we had paid with travelers' checks. We did not have enough money to find a different place to stay. We were stuck! All the manager did was give Larry a vacuum cleaner and some cleaning supplies. They did not even come down to clean the cabin.

We spent our first day of our Colorado honeymoon cleaning. Larry removed the rotten food from the refrigerator and cleaned the kitchen. I vacuumed the carpets in the living room and bedroom that were full of dog hair. Larry went on to scrub the bathroom. We had to go and buy room air fresheners to be able to breathe in the cabin. We burned scented candles at night to help with the smell in the bedroom. We found out that the cabin had been rented for the whole winter to a man who had a dog living with him. He used the woodstove in the living room to warm the cabin all winter. The smell of woodsmoke was mixed in with the dirty-dog smell.

We tried not to be in the cabin very much during our stay in Colorado. We were fortunate because there are so many things to see and do in the Colorado Springs area. The first night, we walked down a rock staircase to the Main Street of Manitou Springs. Fountain Creek runs right through the town. There was a drinking fountain in the town square that flowed with naturally carbonated water that was reputed to have healing powers. Larry remembered coming here to this arcade, while he was in the army. He enjoyed playing the pinball machines. The arcade had old machines that you could play for a nickel or a dime. Larry kept winning free games because he was so good at pinball. I went to a machine where you could print a message on a luck coin. I tried to write "TERRI PACKARD LOVES LARRY ALWAYS." But it was too long, and the letter *T* in my name got left off the coin. The message read, "ERRI PACKARD LOVES LARRY ALWAYS." We had a great time at the arcade.

Reluctantly, we returned to our cabin. We had all the windows wide open in there. It was cleaner in the cabin, but the smell still permeated the atmosphere. Larry held me close, so I did not feel so bad about where we had to stay.

We went to the Air Force Academy and had a tour on the next day. The chapel was beautiful with the sun flooding through the stained-glass windows, making colorful mosaic patterns across the floor. Someone helped Larry and I take a picture of us together under a static B-52 bomber that was painted red, white, and blue at the entrance to the Air Force Academy. We looked around the gift shop and bought something to remember the academy.

That night, we ate at Burger King. This was a real treat for me. A Whopper is my favorite hamburger sandwich. I love the flame broiled taste. I also like to be able to wear a crown. It makes me feel like a princess.

Thursday, we rode the Cog Railway that starts in Manitou Springs to the top of Pikes Peak. It is the world's highest cog road. Along the way, we saw some wildlife that we never saw in Virginia, mule deer, and prairie dogs. We climbed above the tree line in our rail seats. At the top of the mountain, it was cold, and there was snow on the ground. Larry was glad he had his jacket. We went into the gift shop. Larry purchased a souvenir patch to sew on his jacket that said "Cog Railway." We had coffees and doughnuts at the snack bar because we were chilled. Larry started feeling bad. He thought he might be having a heart attack. He was experiencing altitude sickness. Up on Pikes Peak, we were 14,110 feet above sea level. We got on the next car going down the mountain. When we made it back down to Manitou Springs, Larry started feeling better.

MY SMART ROMANCE

We decided to go shopping in the Western shops in Colorado Springs. Both Larry and I bought Western shirts that snapped, closed with pearl buttons. We really liked the snap buttons on the shirts.

Later that day, we did some grocery shopping at the Safeway so we could cook meals and make picnics during the week.

Friday, I went swimming in the little pool at our cabin. It was the best thing about Van Horne. Larry relaxed in a lounge chair by the pool. Larry is not much of a swimmer. When he was young, he and two friends, who were brothers, went out on the Potomac River in a canoe. Larry fell out of the boat. He did not have on a life jacket, and he did not know how to swim. He went under once, twice, and a third time. The older brother grabbed Larry by his hair and hauled him out of the river. Since then, Larry has not been fond of boating or swimming.

That night, we went to the Mason Jar Restaurant in Old Colorado City. This is a landmark in the area. It is a nice family restaurant. The drinks were really served in mason jars. The menu featured comfort foods. We had a pleasant time eating dinner together.

We packed a picnic lunch for Saturday and went to the Garden of the Gods. The red rocks were amazing. We saw the Kissing Camels rock formation at the entrance to the park. We went to one of the gift shops that had a polished big disk that you could look down into and see all around outside the shop. It was amazing. We hiked along some of the trails in the park. We got hungry and ate our sandwiches and apples at one of the picnic tables under a shade tree. We scrambled up rock formations. At the Balancing Rock, I took a picture of Larry that looks like he is holding up that huge rock. He was so strong!

We found a pay phone on Saturday and called home. Remember, this was before cell phone! We had to pay for long-distance calls. Larry talked to his mother. She was doing fine. My parents were not home. They had gone to Virginia Beach in their camper to relax and recuperate after all the work of the wedding, so we did not get to talk to them.

The first day of the week is the Lord's Day. We found a church on Sunday to attend Rustic Hills Baptist Church. Even on our honeymoon, we went to church to worship the Lord. We felt right at home with this congregation of believers. The worship songs warmed our hearts, and the sermon stirred our souls. How wonderful that wherever you go, you can find brothers and sisters in the faith.

Monday, we had a load of dirty laundry to wash, so we made a trip to the laundromat. It is nice that you can do all your loads of clothes at the same time in multiple washers. Then you can dry all the clothes at once. The clothes did not take too long to get clean, dried, and folded. So we toured Old Colorado City. Its Main Street is a tourist destination. Shops with all kinds of tourist needs or wants were lined up and down the thoroughfare. We bought a half pound of fudge at one of the shops. It was so rich and sweet. We had a tour of the Van Briggle Pottery Factory. The building itself was so interesting; it was curved almost like a horseshoe. The pottery and glassware in the factory were beautiful.

We visited Fort Carson on Tuesday. Larry pointed out sites that he remembered from his army days. We went into the museum that honored the Medal of Honor recipients. The stories of their bravery were told and displayed throughout the museum. How amazing the bravery of those men in the face of such dangers. After the museum, we went to Prospect Lake and had a picnic.

Wednesday was the Fourth of July. We spent most of the day at the Garden of the Gods. In the evening, we went to prayer meeting at Rustic Hills Baptist Church. After it got dark, we sat in the car and watched the fireworks in Colorado Springs. We oohed and awed at the spectacular show.

Thursday, we decided we had enough of the stinky cabin. Why suffer any longer? Even though we had paid for another whole week, we wanted to leave. We left Colorado and headed east.

We stopped in Dodge City, Kansas, and visited the Old West Town. We saw a show where cowboys had a shoot-out in the middle of the street. One of the cowboys even fell from a second story balcony when he was shot. We rode on a stagecoach up and down the dirt road in the middle of the town. We had our picture taken by an old locomotive with a caboose. Larry is a great fan of Western movies, so Dodge City was a real treat for him. We drove on east to Great Bend to spend the night.

MY SMART ROMANCE

After our day of driving, on Friday, we stopped at the Columbia Motel in Columbia, Missouri. This was the best hotel of the whole trip, finally a nice place to stay for the night. Larry was resting on the bed, watching a baseball game. This was one of his favorite things to do. I went into the bathroom, had a shower, and put on a little purple teddy. I came out and stretched out on the bed beside Larry. He looked over and said, "How can I pay attention to the ball game with you dressed like that?"

Saturday, we made it to Indianapolis, Indiana. We continued traveling on Sunday. We stopped in Ohio at my Aunt Bessie and Uncle Earl's home and had lunch with them. Then we continued on into the night and finally made it to our apartment in Alexandria, Virginia. We were home. We had traveled 4,182 miles in sixteen days and spent $997.58 on our honeymoon trip to Colorado.

Monday, we slept in. It felt good to have our own place. That night, we went out to dinner at Chi-Chi's, a favorite Mexican restaurant in Springfield, Virginia. The restaurant was in the shopping center, right in front of the apartment complex where I first lived when my family moved to Virginia. I went to school right across the road from that shopping center. I remember, when I was in fourth grade, a radio station had a Thanksgiving stunt. They dropped turkeys from a low flying airplane into the parking lot of that shopping center. It was a very exciting event. I think they later outlawed that practice because it was inhuman to the turkeys.

Larry still had six days before he had to return to work. We decided to finish our honeymoon with a trip to the Delmarva area. We headed for Ocean City, Maryland, on Tuesday. We drove toward the Atlantic Ocean for some sun on the beach. It rained all day! So we just shopped on the boardwalk. We ate caramel corn, crabs, and shrimp. We stayed in a hotel that only had a room for that one night.

When the sun finally came out on Wednesday, we spent time on the beach. I got a terrible sunburn on my shoulders and back. I looked red as a lobster. We found another hotel room for the night. The room had a full bed and a twin bed in it. That night, we laid on the full bed and found out some of the slates were broken under the mattress, and it sagged terribly. (Larry and I did not break the bed!) We could not sleep on that. We tried the twin bed, but I was so sunburned. Through gritted teeth I forceful warned Larry, "*Don't you dare touch me!*"

Finally, we threw the full-size mattress on the floor and laid down on it. We could hear the rain had begun again outside. Then the water started flooding under the door of our hotel room. What could we do? We had water coming up to the mattress we had on the floor—just another adventure for our honeymoon memories.

Thursday, we started back to Alexandria. The traffic was terrible. We moved forward a little then stopped and waited. Then we moved forward a little. The process was repeated over and over. I was not comfortable sitting so long because of my sunburn.

As we were driving, I looked out my passenger window and noticed a convertible driving beside us on the highway. The hair of the man who was driving was flying in the wind. I thought I would not enjoy riding in a convertible with the wind blowing so fast. Larry noticed I was looking out my window. He became jealous. He angrily said, "Stop looking at other men." I was shocked and confused, Larry had no reason to be jealous. I did not want him to think poorly of me.

Written in my journal on July 13, 1984:

> Lord, give me wisdom to know how to act and speak and *look* so I may be pleasing to you and my husband. I need guidance in when I am hurting Larry. Being accused later does not let me prevent the situation. I need to know *when* and *how* to look. Guide me Lord and help me to be obedient. Give me grace and courage.

> Terri

MY SMART ROMANCE

The Bible says in Song of Solomon, "For love is as strong as death, Jealousy as cruel as the grave; Its flames are flames of fire, A most vehement flame."

Dear Heavenly Father,

Please let Larry know he can trust me. I am
faithful to him. My eyes of love are only for him.
Amen.

The Apostle Paul said in 1 Corinthians 7:34, "She who is married cares about...how she may please her husband." I really wanted to please Larry, my new husband.

We were so glad to get back to our little apartment in Alexandria, Virginia. The apartment was clean and smelled good. We had our own queen-size bed that had no broken slats. We had a bedroom without lights flashing on and off all night through the window, a room without rainwater running across the floor toward us. We were where we belonged. Our honeymoon trip was over.

Well, we never will forget our honeymoon adventures! They were truly memorable.

TERRI LYNN SMART PACKARD

Recipe for Honeymoon Salad

Let us alone!

EPILOGUE

Forty Years

June 23, 2024 marks forty years of marriage for Larry and me. We have God to thank for keeping us together all this time. We are two imperfect, sinful people that Jesus has saved. We make mistakes, and we make each other mad. God has given us His grace to share with each other. (Boy, Larry has to give me a lot of grace!) We forgive each other as Christ has forgiven us. We love because Jesus first loved us.

> The preacher and the teacher.
> 40 years filled with smiles and tears.
> Seven children who bring joys and fears.
> Our days slide into years.

Dear Lord,

> Thank You for my husband of forty years. May we continue to serve You together for all the years You give us here on earth.

Love,
Your daughter, Terri

God has given us seven wonderful children. Larry tells me that seven is the number of completion or perfection. We truly have our quiver full. Thank God, He gave each of them to us spread out a bit so we could get used to the added confusion and noise each brought with them:

- Thomas Alexander Packard, born August 1985
- Rebecca Lynn Packard, born June 1987
- Timothy Lee Packard, born November 1988
- Paul Ira Packard, born December 1990
- Rachel Evangeline Packard, born September 1992
- Elizabeth Ellen Packard, born August 1994
- Esther Angel Packard, born April 1997

God has provided every need we had. When raising our children, we could end the month with only five dollars in the bank, but we never were without. We had clothes and food, and we were content. God also gave us a home and vehicles to get around. Our God will supply all your needs. I was able to stay at home and care for our children. People asked, "How can you survive on only one income in Northern Virginia?" We could do this only because God took care of us.

Sometimes God supplied in miraculous ways. I prayed and asked God for some fruit for my children one day.

> Lord,
>
> It would be nice if I had some fruit for my children. Thank You for Your care.
>
> Love,
> Terri

That same day, the lady across the street rang the doorbell and said, "I went to the orchard today and picked apples. I want to share these apples with you." I was amazed.

Another time, I was preparing spaghetti for supper for the nine of us. I checked the cupboard, and we were out of bread. I tried to

MY SMART ROMANCE

think of a way to solve my problem. I could not go to a store and buy bread. I did not have a car to use. I could make biscuits, but I was not very good at that. Larry did not like my biscuits. So I prayed.

Lord,

We have no bread. Please make the spaghetti enough for us.
Amen.

At 5:00 p.m., Larry came through the front door with a big smile on his face. In his hand was a paper bag with long loaves of Italian bread sticking out of the bag. He said, "One of the National Guard men is a baker. He brought all this bread to our shop. He gave me these loaves this morning." Wow! God had answered my prayer even before I prayed. What a wonderful Lord I serve.

When Tom, our oldest child, was to start first grade, Larry said, "You can homeschool him."

I was a high school teacher. What was I supposed to do with a first grader? So we started homeschooling. I was able to homeschool all seven of my children. God had prepared me for that job, and He gave me the ability to do it. Each year was a new challenge. What teaching material to use? How can I have time enough for each child? What adventures could we have as a family? We learned together along the way. My children and I both survived.

When Larry retired from his government job in 2002, we sold our home in Northern Virginia in less than a week. We had to rent back our home so we could live there till Larry was through at Andrews Air Force Base. We packed up everything and moved to Colorado. What an adventure that was. Maybe that is another story I need to write?

When we moved into our Florence, Colorado home, Larry said, "We can live here three years. Then if you don't like it, we can move anywhere you want."

Well, after three years, Larry asked me what I wanted to do. I said, "I like it here. We can stay."

133

TERRI LYNN SMART PACKARD

I married a heavy mobile mechanic, and now I am married to a pastor. Thank God it is the same man, my wonderful husband, Larry Ray Packard. He is still the handsomest man I know. His full head of hair is silver. His mustache is gray. His eyes are lovely blue and sparkle when he beats me in a card game. I still love to hug his neck and smell his great aroma.

> Handsome beyond compare.
> Silver gray of hair,
> Eyes of deepest blue,
> How I Love you!
> Trusting in the Lord.
> The Bible is your sword.
> Each day's adventure is new.
> Oh, How I Love you!

I would like to share seven things that I think are important to life.

1. Prayer. I have always believed in the power of prayer! Since I was a child, I have seen God answer my prayers. God will hear us. God is concerned about the little things in our lives. I want you to know that power. God can do anything!

2. Faith. Put your faith and trust in God alone. People are human, and they will fail you. But God always keeps His promises. Trust in the Lord with all your heart, and He will direct your path. Trust as a little child, nothing doubting or wavering.

3. The Word, God's Word is living. It will speak to your heart's need. It is not old and dry. It has the solutions to problems and the answers to questions. The Bible is sharper than a sword, so be warned: God will cut you to the heart to make you what you need to be.

4. Purpose. Life is only satisfying when you are fulfilling your purpose. Your purpose is to do God's will. You should bring

MY SMART ROMANCE

glory to the Lord in all you say and do. Don't go around being a man pleaser. Please God!

5. Tell the story of Jesus. Do not be ashamed of the Gospel of Christ. Tell what Jesus had done. Tell it at the grocery store. Tell it at the library. Tell it at the park. Tell it to your friends. Tell it to your children. Share the "Good News!"

6. Joy and hope. Have joy in any circumstance. Your hope is in the Lord, who made heaven and earth.

    Smile! Live a joyful life. You do not need to be a pleasure seeker or an epicurean. Find joy in serving others and giving of yourself.

7. Don't limit God. God doesn't fit in our nice, neat box. God is so beyond our understanding. Be ready for God to do big things in your life. God can speak to you! God can open doors, and He can close doors for you! My God specialized in things thought impossible.

I was challenged to write a romance at the Fremont Campus of Pueblo Community College's annual "Senior Mini College" this past year. The class I took as a joke because nothing else was available was "So You Want to Write a Romance." I laughed while signing up for the class because I had no desire to write a romance.

Only three students showed up for the class. The presenter was Andrea K. Stein. She writes spicy romances sold on Amazon. Andrea did a great job sharing about writing a romance. She shared how she got involved in romance writing. She gave us handouts about the genre. She explained about character and setting development. Andrea went through plotting techniques. (I never knew there was a fish-head syndrome.)

Finally, we had a writing exercise. She asked us to write a romantic scene in about ten minutes. Well, the only romance I knew was my own. So I wrote about Larry cooking for me. That started me thinking about Larry and my story. I felt led by the Lord to write it.

So here it is, *My Smart Romance.*

Then and Now

ABOUT THE AUTHOR

Terri is a woman who knows that prayer works. She accepted Jesus as her Savior when she was five years old. She is a pastor's wife who wears many hats at her church. She has homeschooled all seven of her children. For the past twenty-one years, she has been a substitute teacher in the same school district. She loves to teach children. Terri lives in beautiful Colorado. She loves Bible study, painting, and sewing. Terri is a rock hound, who loves looking for rocks.

Printed in the USA
CPSIA information can be obtained
at www.ICGtesting.com
LVHW050148041024
792624LV00002B/326